The Old Testament in the New

☐

an Argument for Biblical Inspiration

Ontario Bible College's
Elmore Harris Series
of Evangelical Books

God and Evil
by William Fitch

Encounter in the Non-Christian Era
by John W. Sanderson, Jr.

*The Old Testament
in Contemporary Preaching*
by Walter C. Kaiser, Jr.

Paul and Jesus
by F. F. Bruce

Emotional Problems and the Gospel
by Vernon Grounds

The Old Testament in the New
by S. Lewis Johnson

The Old Testament in the New

□

an Argument for Biblical Inspiration

S. Lewis Johnson

ZONDERVAN PUBLISHING HOUSE
OF THE ZONDERVAN CORPORATION
GRAND RAPIDS, MICHIGAN 49506

THE OLD TESTAMENT IN THE NEW
Copyright © 1980 by The Zondervan Corporation

Library of Congress Cataloging in Publication Data
Johnson, S Lewis, 1915–
     The Old Testament in the New

     (Contemporary evangelical perspectives)
     Includes index.
     1. Bible—Inspiration—Addresses, essays, lectures.   2. Bible. N.T.—Relation to
O.T.—Addresses, essays, lectures.   3. Typology (Theology)—Addresses, essays,
lectures.   I. Title.
BS480.J63   220.1'3   80-12194
ISBN 0-310-41851-8

Unless otherwise indicated, Scripture quotations are from the New American
Standard Bible, © The Lockman Foundation 1960, 1962, 1963, 1968, 1971, 1972,
1973, 1975.

Edited by Leslie Keylock and Gerard Terpstra
Designed by Gerard Terpstra

Printed in the United States of America

Contents

Foreword

The contemporary climate of biblical exegesis and hermeneutics has produced some very unusual material. Harold Lindsell's *Bible in the Balance* is one of the most recent discussions of the issues, particularly in regard to the inerrancy of the Scriptures.

But the problem of the inspiration, infallibility, and inerrancy of Scripture is not a new discussion. It has been part of the biblical scholar's dialogue ever since the New Testament was completed and gathered with the Old Testament into the canon.

This book by Dr. S. Lewis Johnson, Jr., looks back to the first century and moves forward to the twentieth. The author handles his material with scholarship and skill, stressing both the human and the divine aspects of the problems connected with biblical inspiration.

With spiritual insight he draws together the Old Testament and its New Testament fulfillment.

When Jesus preached, He almost invariably drew from the Old Testament as His authority (cf. Luke 24:25–27), emphasizing that it witnessed to His coming. The symbolism and typology of the Old Testament were all fulfilled in Him.

When Paul wrote his epistles, he also drew from the Old Testament, taking from that record those things that the Holy Spirit wanted him to use and record.

The Scriptures interpret themselves. They are God's Word, and in them He speaks with a unified message.

Dr. Johnson first presented this material at the Thomas F. Staley Academic Lecture Series at Ontario Bible College. The lectures were an enriching experience.

Douglas C. Percy
Ontario Bible College
Willowdale, Ontario, Canada

1

Revelation 19:15 Directly Predictive Messianic Prophecy

INTRODUCTION

Discussions of the inspiration of Scripture in recent years have tended to lay a great deal of emphasis on "an inductive study of the phenomena." By *induction* we mean the method by which one proceeds from observations of particular instances to generalizations about all instances. All logicians admit, of course, that infallibility does not result from induction. In fact, inductive arguments are nondemonstrative and therefore can never claim anything more than probability.[1]

By *phenomena* we mean the historical, chronological, geographical, statistical, and scientific data found in the Bible.

This emphasis on "an inductive study of the phenomena" is not new. Warfield wrote almost a century ago:

> Finally, an effort may be made to justify our holding a lower doctrine of inspiration than that held by the writers of the New Testament, appealing to the so-called phenomena of the Scriptures and opposing these to the doctrine of the Scriptures, with the expectation, apparently, of justifying a modification of the doctrine taught by the Scriptures by the facts embedded in the Scriptures.[2]

Warfield went on to claim that he did not reject the inductive method of establishing doctrine (I personally think he was in error on this point). But he specifically affirmed that every fact indicative of the attitude of the authors of Scripture toward Scripture was relevant to the doctrine of inspiration. He insisted, however, that first and foremost among the phenomena to be investigated are the statements of Scripture concerning its own inspiration and, second only to these, Scripture's use of previous Scripture, especially the use of the Old Testament in the New. Finally, in cases of apparent conflict between the teaching of Scripture regarding its own inspiration and the phenomena of Scripture, it is the phenomena that must give way.[3]

What we will be doing is making a modest attempt to investigate the use of the Old Testament in the New and to relate the conclusions to the present controversy over the doctrine of Scripture.

Revelation 19:15 presents one of the more interesting "phenomena." The apostle John appears at first glance to make use of a text from Psalm 2 in a form that disagrees with the Hebrew text. He speaks (literally) of "shepherding" the nations with a rod of iron, while David wrote of the "breaking in pieces" of the nations with a rod of iron. Let us listen to G. B. Caird's explanation:

> The promise to the Conqueror presents two problems, one linguistic and one theological. It contains an echo—John never quotes verbatim—of Psalm ii. 9, which in the Hebrew runs: "You shall smash them with an iron bar and crush them like an earthenware pot." In the place of the verb "smash" the Septuagint uses *poimainein,* which means either "to be a shepherd" or "to govern"; and John uses this same verb. If we adopt the obvious explanation that John was here using the Septuagint, we should have to conclude that he intended *poimainein* to have one of its normal meanings in Greek usage. But it makes singularly poor sense to say that the Conqueror is "to rule the nations with an iron bar the way earthenware pots are broken," and in any case John does not commonly use the Septuagint, but makes his own, often erratic, translation from the Hebrew. The preferable theory is that John, independently of the Septuagint, made the same mistake which the Septuagint translator had made before him—a perfectly understandable mistake for one to whom Greek was a foreign

language—of supposing that, because the Hebrew r'h can mean both to pasture and to destroy, its Greek equivalent must be capable of bearing both meanings also (cf. xii. 5; xix. 15).⁴*

Professor Caird, then, holds that John erroneously handled the Old Testament, and thus the issue is joined. Did the Beloved Disciple err, and is this phenomenon fundamental for the construction of the biblical doctrine of inspiration?

There are extremes to be avoided in handling such texts. Calvin, for example, committed as he was to an inerrant Scripture, nevertheless admitted that the authors of Scripture were free in their citation. On Romans 3:4 he wrote, "We know that, in quoting Scripture, the apostles often used freer language than the original, since they were content if what they quoted applied to their subject, and therefore they were not over-careful in their use of words."⁵ On Hebrews 10:6 he wrote

> But the Apostle followed the Greek translators when he said, "A body hast thou prepared;" for in quoting these words the apostles were not so scrupulous, provided they perverted not Scripture to their own purpose. We must always have a regard to the end for which they quote passages, for they are very careful as to the main object, so as not to turn Scripture to another meaning; but as to words and other things, which bear not on the subject in hand, they use great freedom.⁶

It is important to note that Calvin was concerned that the words of the citations "applied to their subject," "perverted not Scripture," and "did not turn Scripture to another meaning." In other words, citations may be free in their parts, but they must faithfully represent the meaning of the Old Testament text on the point the New Testament author is making. Thus, the freedom of the New Testament citations is not a perversion of the truth. The meaning the New Testament author finds in the Old Testament text must really be there. Thus, the extreme of erroneous application of Scripture is avoided.

---

*Substantive or explanatory notes are indicated in this text by boldface reference numbers.

On the other hand, the veiwpoint of Francis Turretin, John Henry Heidegger, Luke Gernler, and others, expressed in the *Formula Consensus Helvetica,* that the Hebrew text of the Old Testament was "not only in its consonants, but in its vowels—either the vowel points themselves, or at least the power of the points—not only in its matter, but in its words, inspired of God," is the opposite extreme. No thinking evangelical would affirm a rigid doctrine that included the inspiration of the vowel points of the text, which were devised many centuries after the writing of the *New* Testament.

We will seek to avoid such extremes as we turn to the consideration of the citation of Psalm 2:9 in Revelation 19:15. Did the apostle John err in his citation of the Old Testament? Is the point that he wished to make not really in the Old Testament text to which he alluded? That is the issue.

THE NEW TESTAMENT CONTEXT OF REVELATION 19:15

That the Old Testament is "the Book of the Coming One" is the common knowledge of all who have read it. From the Protevangelium of Genesis 3:15 to the last words of Malachi (cf. 4:2, 5–6) it is occupied with His advent. The necessary and inevitable question, "Where is He?" is purposely, it seems, taken up and answered by Matthew. The Magi came from the East saying, "Where is He who has been born King of the Jews?" (Matt. 2:2), and the first evangelist has taken it upon himself to provide an answer.

W. H. Griffith Thomas, at one time professor of systematic theology at Wycliffe College, Toronto, has contended that a careful study of the Old Testament reveals three great themes of spiritual teaching.

1. It is a book of unfulfilled prophecies from beginning to end.
2. It is a book of unexplained ceremonies. Large amounts of the text are devoted to minute aspects of the cultus, but the Old Testament ends with no full and clear elucidation.
3. It is a book of unsatisfied longings. There is much crying after God and His blessings and, though God responds as the one who initiates all such crying after Him (cf. Rom. 3:11), there is not yet a perfect rest and satisfaction (cf. Heb. 7:18–19; 11:39–40).

In Dr. Thomas's own words,

> It is only when we turn to the New Testament that we find the explanation of all this incompleteness. On the very first page we have the keynote, "That it might be fulfilled," and we are soon able to realise that (a) Jesus Christ the Prophet fulfils (in His life) the prophecies; (b) Jesus Christ the Priest explains (in His death) the ceremonies; and (c) Jesus Christ the King satisfies (in His resurrection) the longings. And so "Jesus, my Prophet, Priest, and King" is the key of the lock, the perfect explanation of the Old Testament and the justification of its spiritual teaching.[7]

Let me express only a minor demurrer. Jesus Christ the King satisfies our longings, not only in His resurrection, but also in His second advent. The New Testament is also "A Book of the Coming One."

John has just concluded his account of the overthrow of the last form of Gentile world power in the collapse of Babylon (see Rev. 17:1–19:10). Now, by means of "seven last things," he will fill in the details. The first is the Messiah's advent, a literal, historical event set forth in symbolic language as the context indicates. The horse is no horse that might be entered in the Kentucky Derby, such as Man of War or Seattle Slew! Nor is the rider a mighty Bellerophon on a marvelous Pegasus sprung from the Gorgon's blood!

The words "And I saw heaven opened" (19:11) introduce the picture of the returning Judge in glory. The horse suggests His warlike character, just as the ass of Zechariah 9:9 suggests His lowliness. The adjectives "Faithful and True" contrast Him with the Beast (cf. 2 Thess. 2:11).

In verse 12 the description of the one whom Swete calls "a royal commander, followed by a dazzling retinue" begins in earnest.[8] Unfortunately we do not have the space to deal with the details.[9]

The reference to the robe dipped in blood[10] must be understood in the light of Isaiah 63:1–6, and the blood in which His robe has been dipped is not His own (He is the slayer here), but that of the kings of the earth (Rev. 17:14) whom he overcomes at His advent.[11] The seventh empire will fall before Him who is responsible for all empires.

The reference to the armies of heaven accompanying the victorious conqueror, probably composed of both angelic beings and the saints of God (cf. Rev. 2:27; 17:14), underscores the picture of the execution of divine wrath by the Messiah. The fact that in the Old Testament it is Yahweh who marches forth to victorious warfare over His enemies presents no problem. The Yahweh of the Old Testament is often the second person of the eternal Trinity. He, too, is Yahweh, as is the Holy Spirit.[12]

But let us not think that the human saints or the angels are responsible for the victory of the Warrior Messiah. It is His conquest alone, as the twofold *autos* ("He"), the intensive pronoun, indicates. In portraying the victory in Revelation 19:15, the apostle draws on some of the greatest messianic sections of the Old Testament. In the first place, "a sharp sword" proceeds from His mouth (cf. Rev. 1:16; 2:12, 16). The reference takes the reader back to Isaiah 49:2 and its description of the words of the Servant of Jehovah as sharp as a sword. In the second place, the clause "so that with it He may smite the nations" comes from Isaiah 11:4, where we read, "And He will strike the earth with the rod of His mouth." That chapter is the climactic unfolding of the Book of Immanuel (Isaiah 7–12) and is strongly messianic. In the third place, the clause "and He will rule them with a rod of iron," as we have seen, comes from Psalm 2:9, a psalm of the messianic King. In the fourth place, the final clause, "and He treads the wine press of the fierce wrath of God, the Almighty," is taken from Isaiah 63:3, set in the context of the final bloody victory of the Warrior Messiah (Servant of Jehovah?). Thus it is clear that the text of the apostle is intended to show that in the final great conflict between heaven and earth it is the work of Immanuel, the Servant of Jehovah, the messianic Warrior King, that is responsible for the victory. The Old Testament is, indeed, "The Book of the Coming One."

It is not surprising, then, that the final statement of the section points the reader to the name that suggests universal sovereignty. It is He, not the despicable Domitian who loved to have himself accorded the name, who is "King of Kings, and Lord of Lords."

The use of Psalm 2:9 in this passage is the part of the text in which we have a special interest. The puzzling feature is the rendering of the verb. The psalm reads, "Thou shalt break them with a rod of iron," but John has, "He will rule [margin: Or shepherd] them with a rod of iron." Now the problem is simply this: The Hebrew text in its Masoretic form has תְּרֹעֵם (NASB "break"), while the Septuagint reads the verb as תִּרְעֵם ("thou shalt shepherd"). John evidently read the Hebrew similarly. The change does not involve any of the consonants of the word, only the vowels. The verb form in the Hebrew text is from רָעַא, "to break," while the form in the Septuagint is evidently from רָעָה, "to shepherd." The change, then, has to do with the vocalization of the Hebrew consonants. The question, however, is this: Did John, whether following the Septuagint or making his own independent translation, err in his use of the Old Testament? (Incidentally, if John erred here, he erred in two other places, for he also cites the line from Psalm 2 in Revelation 2:26–27 and 12:5 [cf. 7:17]).

THE OLD TESTAMENT CONTEXT OF PSALM 2:9

The second Psalm, ascribed to David in Acts 4:25 and much quoted in the New Testament for its high claims for God's Messiah and His universal kingdom, "is unsurpassed for its buoyant, fierce delight in God's dominion and His promise to His King."[13] It is often considered a coronation psalm, but it appears to have been written at a time later than David's accession, when there were no mutinous peoples. The psalm, in my opinion, speaks directly of Jesus Christ by predictive prophecy. The psalmist, perhaps against the background of the accession of a king, is speaking of the *ideal King,* calling Him *Son* on the basis of 2 Samuel 7:14 in the Davidic covenant. Incidentally, history makes no mention of a king of Israel anointed on Zion.[14] It seems clear that the writer of Hebrews read Psalm 2 as a "messianic prediction."[15]

In four scenes the psalmist, plunging immediately into his theme, gives the reader a picture of God's shattering of His enemies through His royal Son. Like a TV camera shifting from one scene to another, the psalm turns first to the raging nations (vv. 1–3), expressing astonishment at the foolish rebellion against the Lord and His Messiah (cf. Acts 4:25–28). Then the camera shifts to heaven, where, in contrast to the wild, rebellious anarchy on earth, the Lord sits in calm contempt (vv. 4–6). The divine derision is masterful. It is as if God were saying, *"You kings* of the earth may revolt, if you stupidly will, *but I* (וַאֲנִי is emphatic) have determined that my King shall reign from Zion, and I will have the last word!"

The camera next shifts to the Son, who claims He is no usurper, but holds His office by divine decree (vv. 7–9). The decree is an enlargement of the promises given to David's heir in the Davidic covenant of 2 Samuel 7:14. The promises look ahead to the resurrection (cf. Acts 13:33; Rom. 1:4) and to the Second Advent, when the nations shall be given to the sovereign Messiah. "Three times," Kidner notes, "the book of Revelation quotes these words, once concerning the victorious Christian (2:27) and twice concerning the Lord (12:5; 19:15)."[16] This kingdom is no kingdom "of the people" and "by the people," although it is "for the people" who are redeemed. The vastness of the dominion promised the Son shows that no king in history could be more than a fleeting shadow of the Messiah.

The camera now moves back to the earth, and the mutinous nations are offered their only hope. It is total submission to the Son,[17] the only way to escape God's wrath.

One can easily see how appropriate is the use of this psalm, especially verses 8 and 9, in the context of the overthrow of the kings of the earth's nations at the second coming of Christ. On the fiery picture of the last strophe Kidner comments, "That is, God's patience is not placidity, any more than His fierce anger is loss of control, His laughter cruelty or His pity sentimentality."[18]

The Comparison of the Old and New Testament Texts

For purposes of comparison I have set out the texts of the Greek New Testament text (the United Bible Societies edition), the Greek Old Testament (LXX—the Septuagint text of Rahlfs), and the Hebrew Old Testament (MT—the Masoretic text).

NT	LXX	MT
(Rev. 19:15)	(Ps. 2:9)	(Ps. 2:9)
ποιμανεῖ αὐτοὺς ἐν ῥάβδῳ σιδηρᾷ	ποιμανεῖς αὐτοὺς ἐν ῥάβδῳ σιδηρᾷ	תְּרֹעֵם בְּשֵׁבֶט בַּרְזֶל
He will shepherd them with a rod of iron.	Thou shalt shepherd them with a rod of iron.	Thou shalt break them with a rod of iron.

COMMENTS ON VARIATIONS IN THE TEXTS

We are dealing with an implicit citation from the Old Testament. While there is no introductory citation formula, the allusion to Psalm 2:9 is clearly intentional. As a matter of fact, although it has been estimated that of the 404 verses of the Apocalypse 278 contain references to the Old Testament, there is not one formal citation from the Old Testament in the book.[19] Many of the allusions, however, are intended as citations (see, for example, Rev. 2:26–27; 12:5).

The Old Testament text cited by the author is similar to that of the Septaugint, but he rarely uses the *ipsissima verba* (the exact words) of the Old Testament. His custom is ordinarily to modify the Old Testament passage or to combine features from several passages into one. His work is that of a creative mind full of Scripture, and a master of its meaning.

In these texts there are only two variations. In the New Testament the verb is in the third person. John has woven it into the context of his unfolding of the vision, which is given in the third person. The difference is of no great significance.

The second variation has been referred to previously in this chapter, the variation between "break" and "shepherd" or "rule."

That brings us to the heart of the problem of the use of the Old Testament in Revelation 19:15. How are we to explain the variation of the New Testament text from the Old Testament Masoretic text? Let me suggest the following conclusions:

1. That the Masoretic text is the original text has not been universally accepted. As Old Testament textual critics know, the Septuagint in quite a few places appears to preserve superior readings.

At this very place the reading of the Septuagint is supported by the Syriac Peshitta, the Vulgate, and Jerome. The Vulgate's reading is *reges*, "thou shalt rule." In fact, the reading of the Septuagint is more suited to the word *rod*, or *sceptre*, even if it should be of iron (cf. Ps. 23:4; 45:7).[20] On the other hand, the parallelism favors the reading of the Masoretic text. I mention these points not to solve the question of the text but simply to note that it is possible, although not likely, that the Masoretic reading is not genuine. If it should not be, the alleged problem would evaporate.

2. That the apostle has simply borrowed the reading ποιμαίνει from the Septuagint is doubtful. He does not ordinarily borrow from the Septuagint. His renderings, as a rule, indicate that he handled the Hebrew text independently.[21] It is, of course, possible, since he knew the Septuagint, that he recognized in its rendering here a brilliant, ironical figure of speech. To shepherd with a rod of iron would emphasize that aspect of the shepherd's work in which he guarded his flock from enemies. In fact, the shepherd's rod was an oaken club of a formidable nature, fit for a ruler's sceptre (cf. Gen. 49:10).[22] The sense of the destruction of the flock's enemies would be present in the rendering of both the Septuagint and the Masoretic text. Thus if John borrowed the word from the Septuagint, it may well have been because he saw the suitability and the validity of its meaning. This, of course, is something we cannot be sure of in the light of our present knowledge.

3. R. H. Charles in his massive commentary on the Apocalypse has suggested that John gave ποιμαίνειν two distinct meanings. He writes, "A comparison of xix. 15, where ποιμανεῖ is parallel to πατάξῃ, and of the present text, ii. 27, where it is parallel with συντρίβεται (cf. also xii. 5), is strong evidence that our author attached two distinct meanings to ποιμαίνειν."[23] The fact that he gave the word two meanings is supported by the renderings of the Vulgate and the Syriac versions, both of which render the verb by "to rule" instead of "to shepherd." The common meaning is found in 7:17, but the meaning "to devastate, lay waste" is found in 2:27, 12:5, and 19:15.

How did John come to this conclusion, since it does not seem to be found outside of biblical Greek? Perhaps he did so because ποιμαίνειν is found in the Septuagint chiefly for רָעָה, "to shepherd." In fact, it is found over forty times as a rendering of this word. The Hebrew word usually means "to shepherd," but it also means "to destroy" or "to devastate" (cf. Micah 5:6 [v. 5 in the Hebrew Bible], וְרָעוּ אֶת־אֶרֶץ אַשּׁוּר בַּחֶרֶב). The same is true of the word in Jeremiah 2:16 (ASV, RSV "broken"), 22:22 (NASB "sweep away"), and Psalm 80:14 (in which it is parallel to כִּרְסֵם [kirsem], meaning "to ravage, gobble"). In Micah 5:6, Jeremiah 6:3, and 22:22 the Septuagint has rendered רָעָה by ποιμαίνειν, evidently giving it the sense of "to devastate." We may conclude, then, that, in the light of the parallel with πατάσσω (NASB "smite") in 19:15, ποιμαίνειν has been given by John the meaning of "to destroy," or "devastate."[24] The use of the phrase "with a rod of iron" supports the meaning. What, then, becomes of the claim that John made a mistake? It is groundless.[25]

JOHN'S HERMENEUTICAL USE OF THE OLD TESTAMENT

The apostle John has read Psalm 2 as a directly predictive psalm, one that looks on to the second advent of the Messiah, when He will come again to establish the messianic Kingdom on the earth. There may be some sense, by way of application, in which this promise is fulfilled in the present life of believers (cf. Acts 4:23–31), but the primary force of the text is eschatological, looking to the Parousia.[26] The victory of the Messiah will be shared by His people (see Rev. 2:26–27).

JOHN'S THEOLOGICAL USE OF THE OLD TESTAMENT

The four passages that John leans on in the composition of Revelation 19:15 are Isaiah 49:2; Isaiah 11:4; Psalm 2:9; and Isaiah 63:3. A careful study of the contexts of these passages leads to an interesting conclusion. The first passage occurs in the second of the Servant of Yahweh songs, while the second is found near the climax of the Book of Immanuel and is part of the description of the conquest and rule of the Shoot from the stem of Jesse. The third passage is descriptive of the conquest of the nations by the King, who has been anointed by the Lord. The final passage is from the vivid dialogue between the prophet and the mighty Conqueror of the nations from Bozrah. The victor is none other than Yahweh who in wrath treads down the nations in the day of His vengeance (cf. Luke 4:14–21). It is very striking that each of the passages is messianic, looking ahead to the coming Redeemer, and eschatological, pointing to the second advent of the Conqueror. It is then that the King, who has suffered, shall take over the reins of human government, establishing His kingdom over the earth. These passages present a unified picture of Yahweh, the Second Person of the eternal Trinity.

CONCLUSION

How fitting it is, then, that the paragraph concludes with the mention of His name as "King of Kings and Lord of Lords." Three times in the section He is given a name, once for Himself alone (v. 12), once in reference to the redeemed (v. 13), and once in reference to the entire cosmos (v. 16). All people are able to read it, for all will live under His dominion.

Reinhold Niebuhr wrote, "It is unwise for Christians to claim any knowledge of either the furniture of heaven or the temperature of hell; or to be too certain about any details of the Kingdom of God in which history is consummated."[27] The words are a valid warning against prophetic sensationalism, of which there is too much today. But at the same time the Apocalypse does shed light on the future, and its content is trustworthy. The infallible Word assures us that Watts was right when he wrote,

> Jesus shall reign where'er the sun
>   Does his successive journeys run;
> His kingdom stretch from shore to shore
>   Till moons shall wax and wane no more.

2

John 10:34–36
The Problem
of the Phenomena

In the preceding chapter I pointed out that one of the most salutary features of New Testament study today is its emphasis on the importance of the Old Testament for New Testament studies. A prominent New Testament scholar wrote some time ago, "After ransacking all sorts of sources, Jewish and Greek (and, we may add, starting all sorts of 'hares,' some of which have not run very well), they [the scholars] are rediscovering the truth of Augustine's dictum, 'The New Testament lies hidden in the Old, and the Old is made plain in the New.'"[1]

R. W. Dale, a distinguished Congregationalist scholar of the nineteenth century, wrote, "The institutions of the Old Testament are to a large extent a dictionary in which I learn the true sense of the language of the New."[2]

And more recently a Continental scholar has said, "The Old Testament is the true Bible, and the New Testament is its explanatory glossary."[3]

"We cannot remind ourselves too often," T. W. Manson declared, "that the Bible of the Apostolic Church was the Old Testament; and that it was to the Old Testament that the first Christians turned for guidance on all matters of faith and conduct."[4]

I cannot help but feel that the apostles and the other authors of the New Testament would have agreed heartily with these sentiments. We cannot hope to make further progress in the understanding of the biblical revelation if we fail to concentrate a significant amount of our attention on the influence the Old Testament has had on the New.

To illustrate the relevance of this discipline, let me mention just a few of the contemporary questions that are influenced by the conclusions we draw from the use of the Old Testament in the New. First of all, it is well known that one of the major questions before New Testament students today is the question of the authenticity of the words of Jesus in the Gospels. By using certain criteria of authenticity, the chief of which is the "criterion of dissimilarity," it is claimed that much of the teaching of Jesus may come from the early church, and not from Him at all. For example, if a saying displays the thoughts or concerns of the primitive church, then we cannot be sure it is authentic, i.e., that it comes from Jesus. And, further, if the saying is such that a Jew of the period could have said it, then it may be a piece of popular teaching put into the mouth of our Lord.[5] Additions to this criterion have been proposed by others,[6] but it is unnecessary for us to pursue the matter in more detail here. The important thing to note is that the criterion has been used to make the absurd claim that, if anyone else could have said it, Jesus could not have! The weakness of such a conclusion philosophically, methodologically, and historically is patent.

There is, however, a further test to which the criterion of authenticity may be put, namely, the test from the data of the use of the Old Testament in the New. If the picture obtained from the use of the Old Testament in the New is a coherent and consistent whole, reflecting the work of original minds, and if it can be shown that the way Jesus uses the Old Testament differs from the way the early church used it in its preaching and writing, we may conclude that those passages in the Gospels that reflect our Lord's use of the Old Testament are, in fact, authentic.[7] In this book I do not investigate the question in detail, but I am confident from my study that the conclusion that could be drawn would give strong support to the case for the authenticity of the words of Jesus in our Gospels.

Second, the use of the Old Testament in the New is the key to the solution of the problem of hermeneutics. Unfortunately that has been overlooked, but surely, if the apostles are reliable teachers of biblical doctrine, then they are reliable instructors in the science of hermeneutics. And what better way is there to discover their hermeneutics than to investigate their use of the Old Testament Scriptures?

Third, the use of the Old Testament in the New is of significance in the continuing debate over the deity of Christ. To give a simple illustration, is it not of great importance that in the Book of Revelation, that "gorgeous picture-book,"[8] many of the most sublime titles for deity are applied to Jesus Christ by the apostle John? It should not surprise us that the christology of Revelation is of an advanced character, being perhaps the highest found in the New Testament (cf. Rev. 1:8; 22:13; Isa. 44:6).

Fourth, for the doctrine of typology it is obvious that we must rely on the New Testament viewpoint for the way we go about discovering types in the Old Testament.

Fifth, even for such a "hot" contemporary issue as the biblical teaching about women the use of the Old Testament in the New is crucial. Is it really true, as Paul K. Jewett has claimed, that Paul's views on the subject, taken ostensibly from the Old Testament, are self-contradictory? Was he wrong, as a rabbi, but did he gain some liberating insights as a Christian? Was the apostle's exegesis of a kind that "defies hermeneutical ingenuity," and was it "problematic"?[9] Was he right in Galatians 3:28, but wrong when handling Genesis 1–2? We would not contend that Luther's note to his friend Stephen Roth was in the spirit of the New Testament. It began, "Grace and peace in Christ and authority over your wife." Nor was Diana Barrymore right in insisting, "Every woman ought to be struck regularly, like a gong." On the other hand, the apostolic exegesis of the Old Testament on the subject of women leads clearly to the conclusion that the equality of the sexes in Christ is not contradictory to the subordination of the female to the male in the home and in the church.

Sixth, the question of whether the Old Testament is to be spiritualized in its prophetic portions can be answered only by a careful study of the use the apostles make of those portions in the New Testament. Thus, no solution to the postmillennial-amillennial-premillennial controversy can ever be reached apart from a satisfactory handling of this aspect of the question.

Finally, the biblical doctrine of inspiration can never be adequately constructed apart from a convincing handling of the use of Scripture by our Lord and the apostles.

This last subject is particularly relevant because of the present controversy among evangelicals over the doctrine of inspiration. Incidentally, I am using the term *evangelical* of those who are fully committed to Protestant orthodoxy, whether of the Lutheran, Reformed, Anglican, or Anabaptist expression. Among these believers the doctrine of the inspiration of the Scriptures, especially of the inerrancy of the Scriptures, has become the most sensitive of all issues. I agree, of course, with Kenneth S. Kantzer that inerrancy

> should not be made a test for Christian fellowship in the body of Christ. The evangelical watchcry is "Believers only, but all believers." Evangelicals did not construct the church and do not set its boundaries. Christ is Lord and he is Lord over his church. The bounds of fellowship are determined by our relationship to Christ and by the life we share in him by grace through faith alone.[10]

Kantzer's words contain a salutary admonition and they should be kept before us in the heat of the debate.

Simply stated, the doctrine of inerrancy is that everything the Bible asserts is true. Among evangelicals at the present time there are, broadly speaking, three viewpoints concerning this doctrine.

The first evangelical viewpoint is that represented by Dewey M. Beegle, whose *Scripture, Tradition, and Infallibility*[11] is "an all-out, no-holds-barred, always aggressive, sometimes insidious attack"[12] on the full truthfulness of the Word of God. The fundamental contention of Beegle is that there are incontrovertible errors in the

Bible.[13] We cannot, of course, examine his biblically and philosophically flawed work here, but it is clear that Beegle attempts to prove by subjective criteria that the Word of God errs. Beegle believes, then, that the Bible is errant, but that it is still "in all essential matters of faith and practice . . . authentic, accurate, and trustworthy."[14] While I am not charging them with the faulty and fallacious reasoning of Beegle, in his camp belong such names as G. C. Berkouwer, F. F. Bruce, and Paul K. Jewett.

The second evangelical viewpoint is that represented by Daniel P. Fuller, Bernard Ramm, David Hubbard, Stephen T. Davis, Harry R. Boer, and others. It is Fuller's contention that the Bible contains material that is revelatory and other material that is nonrevelatory. The latter material functions as an aid to the transmission of the revelatory material. The revelatory matter is that which is intended to make us "wise unto salvation." It is Fuller's contention that the Bible is inerrant in its revelatory material and that it is proper to speak of the Bible as inerrant, since it is true to its purpose.[15] Since, however, he does admit the strong probability of errors in matters of history, geography, and science, his view has been called "the limited inerrancy viewpoint," or "partial inerrancy."[16]

Finally, there are those who continue in the tradition of Benjamin Breckenridge Warfield, claiming also the support of the early Fathers, including Augustine, Luther, and Calvin, who contend that the Bible is fully inspired and free from all error in its teaching. Those who hold this position affirm that the biblical writers may use paraphrases, summaries, figures of speech, metaphors, hyperbole, and the like. In making citations from the Old Testament, the New Testament writers need not give completely accurate renderings, if the sense the New Testament author finds in the Old Testament passage is really there. Among those on the contemporary scene who hold this view are James Montgomery Boice, John H. Gerstner Kenneth S. Kantzer, John Warwick Montgomery, James I. Packer, and R. C. Sproul. Of course, Harold Lindsell, whose *Battle for the Bible* caused such a stir, also belongs to this third group.

The "summit" conference, sponsored by the International Council on Biblical Inerrancy and held in Chicago, October 26-28,

1978, produced a Short Statement that sought to articulate the traditional inerrancy position, together with nineteen articles of affirmation and denial. The Short Statement contains the words that epitomize its position: "Scripture is without error or fault in all its teaching." Four-fifths of the three hundred evangelicals who attended the conference signed the Chicago Statement on Biblical Inerrancy.

A question that keeps emerging in the debate over inerrancy is the problem of the phenomena. By *phenomena* is meant, not the statements of the Bible about its inspiration, such as 2 Timothy 3:16–17 and 2 Peter 1:20–21, but specific historical, chronological, scientific, and geographical data. And to the data is to be added the facts that surface from a study of the use that the New Testament authors make of the Old Testament in their citations and allusions. In other words, the biblical doctrine of inspiration is not to be constructed simply by an exegesis of the normative texts that affirm inspiration but also by a consideration of the other data found in the Bible, that is, the phenomena.

We cannot deny that in the construction of the biblical doctrine of inspiration we must use the express statements of Scripture regarding its inspiration and all the other relevant data, such as the phenomena. Without affirming the inspiration of the inductive method (one can never arrive at the certainty of any truth by its use)—we nevertheless insist that an inductive investigation of the subject of inspiration must include a consideration of both the express statements of Scripture and the phenomena. But we further insist that the express statements must always take precedence over the phenomena, for the same reason that the clear statements of Scripture concerning a particular teaching always take precedence over the less clear ones. Just as the acts of God, such as the events of the Exodus, need the biblical statements for their elucidation, so the phenomena of Scripture need the explicit statements of Scripture concerning inspiration for their explanation.[17]

In the final analysis, to satisfy the critics of the traditional view of inspiration it would be necessary to handle *all* the phenomena *perfectly*. That I cannot do. This book is directed to one aspect of the problem of the phenomena, namely, the use of the Old Testament in the New Testament and its relation to the doctrine of inspiration. And it is only a modest attempt; the subject is a mammoth one. There are over three hundred explicit quotations of the Old Testament in the New, and there are literally thousands of allusions. To handle the problem fully would consume a lifetime. The basic method of approach, however, is a rather simple and consistent one, even though the results of its application vary widely. It is my intention to turn to several of the significant uses of the Old Testament in the New Testament in order to illustrate both the method we must follow in the solution of this aspect of the problem of the phenomena and some of the problems and some usages that are unfolded in the exegesis of the apostles. But, remember, what we see are only "some" of the usages, and the problems we face and attempt to solve are only "some" of the types of problems found in the text.

The question constantly before us is this: What do the New Testament authors think of the Old Testament? Further, what adjectives would they find useful in describing it? I suggest that they hold the Old Testament to be historical revelation, strongly messianic in content, often predictive and typical in its forward look, and always inspired and inerrant in its teaching.

After this lengthy introduction let us now turn to our first illustrative passage, John 10:22-39. It contains our Lord's discourse to the Jews at the Feast of Dedication and includes a very important comment on the Scripture.

THE NEW TESTAMENT CONTEXT OF JOHN 10:34-36

John 10, the chapter on the Good Shepherd, contains two discourses. The first is composed of three parables (vv. 1-21); the second contains two addresses by our Lord (vv. 22-30, 31-39). At the conclusion of the first address Jesus claims absolute unity with the Father.[18] The remarkable statement "I and the Father are one" (lit. "one thing") contradicts the claims the Sabellians made centuries later, for they denied that there are three persons in the Trinity and argued that these were only modes of manifestation of the deity. The plural *esmen* (Gr. ἐσμέν, AV "are") denotes plurality of persons. It also is incompatible with Arianism, which denied the deity of the Son in affirming His creation. The neuter, "one thing," may not have a metaphysical force here, but Morris is surely right in saying, "It is also true that it means more than that Jesus' will was one with the Father's."[19] The Jews would hardly have tried to stone Him to death for blasphemy for making such a claim. The fact that they did try clearly suggests that they knew He had made a claim to deity.

"They had asked Jesus for a plain assertion of His messiahship," Morris says, "and they got more than they had bargained for."[20] The reaction that His statement produced made it necessary that He address them further. Thus He asked the reason for the attempted stoning and received the reply that it was for blasphemy. He had made Himself out to be God (cf. vv. 31–33). That claim, of course, they never bothered to investigate; they assumed it was false.

The Lord's response is an appeal to Scripture to justify His claim to be *one with the Father,* and to be His *Son* (cf. vv. 25, 29–30). The citation is from Psalm 82:6, which in its entirety reads, "I said, 'You are gods, and all of you are sons of the Most High.'" The force of the words is that the Jewish Scriptures indicated that men who became judges by divine appointment consequently possessed a certain limited measure of divinity. In effect, they stood in God's place (cf. v. 1). This is sufficient to show the possibility of a perfect union of God with man, and Jesus claims to be the individual who has realized this perfect union, for He is God's Son (vv. 34–36).

In the final words of the section Jesus appeals to His works in support of this union. He does not utter blasphemy; it is simple demonstrable truth (vv. 37–39). He hopes that, when they see that He does the works of His Father, they will come to know (aorist tense) and continue knowing (present tense) the mutual indwelling of the Father and the Son.

This is a simple statement of the movement of thought through the section. The details of the text, particularly those connected with the use of the psalm, are not so easy.

Coleridge, it is said, once told Robert Browning that he could not understand all his poetry. "Ah, well," replied the poet, "if a reader of your calibre understands ten per cent of what I write, he ought to be content." And when Wordsworth was told that Browning had married Elizabeth Barrett, he is reported to have said, "It is a good thing that these two understand each other, for no one else understands them."

A pupil once brought to Hegel a passage from the philosopher's own writings and asked him for an interpretation. The philosopher examined it and replied, "When that passage was written, there were two who knew its meaning—God and myself. Now, alas, there is but one, God."

It is not so with us. The Scriptures were written for our understanding, and the Holy Spirit was given to "guide the church into all the truth" (John 16:13). Therefore we have the right to examine the Word of God and to expect that God's meaning will be made clear to us. Before we can reach some supportable conclusions, we must look at the text in its Old Testament setting.

THE OLD TESTAMENT CONTEXT OF PSALM 82:6

Psalm 82 has been entitled, "The Judgment of Unjust Judges or Rulers."[21] Asaph, the author, writes of theocratic judges, although attempts have been made to see the psalm as referring to heathen gods, heathen rulers, or even angels.[22] I am inclined to think that Exodus 22:28 (cf. vv. 8–9; 21:6) is sufficient evidence for the use of *Elohim,* the Hebrew name used in verses 1 and 6 for "judges" (cf. 1 Chron. 29:23; Deut. 1:17; 2 Chron. 19:6–7).

Very briefly the psalm contains: (1) an indictment (vv. 1–5), (2) a verdict (vv. 6–7), and (3) a plea (v. 8).[23] In the verdict is the citation with which we are concerned. God acknowledges that He has given the judges the position of administrators of His justice (v. 6a) and has made them the objects of His love (v. 6b). But the judges will die the death of ordinary men because they have judged unjustly (cf. Judg. 16:7, 17). The psalm applies to earthly rulers today, who are also "ministers of God" (cf. Rom. 13:1–7).

THE COMPARISON OF THE OLD AND NEW TESTAMENT TEXTS

In addition to the Greek New Testament, the Septuagint, and the Hebrew Old Testament, we will use also the Old Testament Targum.

The New Testament introductory formula (IF) by which the citation is introduced into the text, is also given.

NT	LXX	MT
(John 10:34)	(Ps. 82:6)	(Ps. 82:6)

IF: οὐκ ἔστιν γεγραμμένον ἐν τῷ νόμῳ ὑμῶν ὅτι

ἐγὼ εἶπα· θεοί ἐστε;

ἐγὼ εἶπα θεοί ἐστε καὶ υἱοὶ ὑψίστου πάντες.

אֲנִי־אָמַרְתִּי
אֱלֹהִים אַתֶּם
וּבְנֵי עֶלְיוֹן
כֻּלְּכֶם:

Targum

(Ps. 82:6)

אֲנָא אֲמָרִית הֵי
כְמַלְאֲכַיָּא אַתּוּן הֲשִׁיבִין
וְהֵיךְ אַנְגְלֵי
מְרוֹמָא כּוּלְכוֹן

IF: "Has it not been written in your Law,

'I said you are gods?'"

I said, "You are gods, and all of you sons of the Most High."

I said, "You are gods, and all of you sons of the Most High."

I said, "You were regarded just as angels, and you all just as angels on high."

COMMENTS ON VARIATIONS IN THE TEXTS

The text of the New Testament agrees exactly with the text of the Septuagint, and the latter is an exact equivalent of the Hebrew text.

The Targum is quite different from the Hebrew, and it has been suggested that its rendering may have arisen out of a desire to avoid any suggestion of human equality with God.[24] It is important to remember, however, that the Jews of Jesus' day, when they heard His citation of the text, did not question His interpretation or see the quotation as a reference to human beings.

JESUS' HERMENEUTICAL USE OF THE OLD TESTAMENT

The use that the Lord Jesus makes of Psalm 82:6 has been debated, and we need to consider it at this point. There are two questions that we must answer. First, to what does the term "gods" refer in Psalm 82:6? And second, what is the force of our Lord's argument in John 10:34–36?

First, then, to what does the term "gods" refer in Psalm 82:6 (cf. v. 1)? In Judaism three senses have been suggested. A fragment of a scroll from Cave 11 at Qumran contains an exposition of part of Psalm 82, and in it the word *elohim*, "gods," is referred to the evil angels. J. A. Emerton has accepted the reference to the angels in the fragment as confirmatory of his own view that the psalmist was referring to the evil angels. Thus, according to Emerton, our Lord's argument would not be based on the fact that men are called "gods" but more generally on the idea that "gods" may refer to beings other than God to whom He has committed authority, namely, in this case, the angels. Emerton's view, however, suffers from two defects. In the first place, it is contrary to the context of the psalm. There is no clear reference to angels in the psalm, while there are clear references to men (cf. vv. 3–4, 5, 7–8). Moreover, Jesus' argument would lack force if the word referred to angels. The whole point He is making is that certain *men* may be called *gods*. Thus, in the light of who He is, it is not strange that He, a *man,* should claim to be the Son of God, or *God.*[25]

Anthony Hanson has suggested that the psalm is addressed by the preexistent Word of God to the Jews on Mount Sinai at the giving of the Law. Thus, in John 10:34–36 it is the incarnate Word of God who addresses their descendants. He adds, "The hearing of the Law was to make them immortal, but the episode of the golden calf manifested their disobedience whereby they and all their posterity lost the gift of immortality." This tradition is found in the rabbis.

It is true that rabbinic tradition sees the psalm as addressed to Israel or some part of Israel, as Hanson claims, but it would be difficult (I think impossible) to support from Scripture the calling of all the Israelites at Sinai "gods." Therefore, I cannot follow this novel view.

While a number of contemporary interpreters refer the term to heavenly gods,[26] it is more in harmony with the context and the analogy of Scripture to refer the term to human judges, appointed by God as His representatives in the administration of justice in Israel (cf. Exod. 21:6; 22:7–8, 28; Deut. 1:17; 1 Chron. 29:23; 2 Chron. 19:6–7).

That brings us to the second question, namely, what is the force of our Lord's argument? We shall consider several answers.

1. A common view is that expressed by the late J. N. Sanders: "Jesus appeals to Scripture to clear himself of the charge of blasphemy, and again uses the typically rabbinic form of argument *from light to heavy* (cf. vii. 22 f.)."[27] One of Hillel's famous norms of hermeneutics, the *qal wahomer* argument refers to an inference *a fortiori,* or *a minori ad maius,* "for a still stronger reason," "all the more." The point of Jesus' reply is simply that, since the Scriptures calls the judges "gods," and they were mere men, much more may the term be applied to One whom the Father sanctified and sent into the world. To Sanders, however, the argument is a mere *ad hominem* argument, one that the Jews might find plausible, but one that others schooled in historical criticism would find unconvincing. The reason he finds the argument unconvincing is that he has failed to notice the force of the relative clause in verse 36, "whom the Father sanctified and sent into the world," a clause that marks Him out as unique among men. Jesus' argument is not that Psalm 82:6 refers to men as gods and that He is therefore not blaspheming in calling Himself God, for He is a man, too. His argument would in that case prove too much, for it would make the dignity He claimed a common dignity, not one that was exclusive and unique.[28] The claims of the relative clause are necessary, giving validity to the argument. Otherwise, as Bernard says, "the argument

is insecure, because it seems to pass from 'gods' in the lower sense to 'God' in the highest sense of all."[29]

2. B. B. Warfield, thinking that there is a vein of satire in our Lord's words throughout the section, has contended that the argument is not *ad hominem,* acceptable on Jewish principles, but *e concessu,* by concession. Scripture is common ground for Him and His opponents, and He is simply pointing out that they were willing to admit that corrupt judges might be called "gods," but were unwilling, in fact could not endure, that He, sanctified and sent into the world by the Father, should call Himself Son of God.[30]

3. Several commentators on the Gospel of John have pointed to a deeper meaning contained in our Lord's argument.[31] There is more in it than contention for a *word,* although that is important. He has made the astounding claim of absolute unity with the Father (cf. vv. 30, 38). Following this He argues *a fortiori* in a form that may be expressed in a syllogism as follows:

Major premise: The Scripture cannot be broken.

Minor premise: The Scripture spoke of men *to* whom the Word of God came as *gods.*

Conclusion: Jesus, sanctified and sent forth as the Word of God into the world by God, is rightly called *God* in a correspondingly higher sense.[32]

It is an argument *a minori ad maius,* but basic to our Lord's thought is the idea of the union of God and man (cf. vv. 30, 38 again). This idea is implied in the relationship that God had with the judges in the Old Covenant days. They were gods because He by His word that appointed them had entered into a *relationship of limited union* with them (cf. Ps. 82:1). They stood in His place and were types and shadows of a deeper union to come. "The strict Hebrew doctrine of God left no place for the Incarnation. God and man were set over against each other, as wholly separate and distinct," Bernard wrote, adding, "But even in the Jewish Scriptures there are hints and foreshadowings of potential divinity in man (cf. Ps. 82[6], Zech. 12[8]); and it is to this feature of Hebrew theology that attention is drawn in v. 34."[33] In other words, the germ of the union of God and man is found in the Law.[34]

The relative clause of verse 36 adds the necessary facts that substantiate His argument. They show that His claim for a *perfect realization of union* is grounded in eternal truths and the heavenly commission. The sanctifying, or setting apart, was for the divine task of revelation and atonement and included all the necessary endowment of powers (cf. John 6:69; 17:19). The sending followed as the final and complete union of God and man in activity among men. The Incarnation and the Atonement, therefore, were the aim of all the Old Testament revelation. Since the *Father* sent Him, and since He perfectly realized the union of God and man, it is right and proper that He call Himself *the Son of God,* in whom is the Father and who is in the Father (cf. Isa. 9:6–7; Gal. 4:4–5). The Incarnation, then, contrary, not to monotheism, but to false Jewish Anti-Trinitarian monotheism, was not alien to the spirit of the Old Testament Scriptures. It was, in fact, set forth clearly in typical anticipations.

To summarize, then, the hermeneutical use of the Old Testament by our Lord is that of *typical fulfillment.*

JESUS' THEOLOGICAL USE OF THE OLD TESTAMENT

In the final section of this chapter we turn to some of the theological truths that emerge from our Lord's handling of the Old Testament Scriptures. They are significant for some of the theological controversies of our day.

1. We find in John 10:34–36 plain indications of our Lord's attitude to the authority of the Scriptures. He refers to them as "Law" (Gr. $\nu \acute{o} \mu o \varsigma$), and it is the opinion of the mass of biblical commentators that this word here refers to the whole of the Old Testament. It certainly does not refer only to the five books of Moses (cf. 8:17), for the citation is from the Psalms. The reference to $\nu \acute{o} \mu o \varsigma$ as the whole of the Old Testament is not uncommon in the New Testament nor in the rabbinic writings.[35] In fact, there are three terms that are used for the entirety of Scripture: 1. "Law" (cf., e.g., 1 Cor. 14:21; John 12:34; 15:25), 2. "Scripture" (cf. John 10:35, where the word is synonymous with "Law," according to Warfield[36]; 2:22; 7:38), and 3. "prophecy" (cf. 2 Peter 1:19–21).

Now it is important to notice that Jesus' defense is an appeal to "your Law," and to that Law in its written form. He does not appeal to the text because it is in the Psalms, but because it is in the *body of writings* called the "Law." "In other words," as Warfield notes, "He here ascribes legal authority to the entirety of Scripture, in accordance with a conception common enough among the Jews (cf. John xii. 34), and finding expression in the New Testament occasionally, both on the lips of Jesus Himself, and in the writings of the apostles."[37] What we have here, then, is "the strongest possible assertion of the indefectible authority of Scripture."[38] To put it another way, as our Lord does in verse 35, "The Scripture cannot be broken." That clause was not necessary for the validity of His argument, but it does serve the purpose of giving a clear statement of our Lord's attitude to the Word of God.

The word "broken" is used by John for the breaking of the Law or the Sabbath (John 5:18; 7:23; cf. Matt. 5:19). Its force is simply that the Scripture cannot be "annulled,"[39] or "emptied of its force by being shown to be erroneous."[40] Its teaching cannot be abrogated. Is it pressing the point to say that it is inerrant in everything it asserts?

2. We find in this passage a clear indication of our Lord's attitude to the inspiration of the Scriptures. There are two things to note. In the first place, the clause, "I said, you are gods," is not a very important clause; in fact, if our Lord had not cited it, we might wonder, if we were among those who feel that Scripture is inspired only in that which has to do with faith and practice, if it really belonged to the part of the Bible to which we must yield submission. It is such an incidental statement, and its meaning is in scholarly doubt. And yet it is this incidental statement, and even its incidental form, that the Lord Jesus says cannot be broken! Warfield has said it better than anyone else:

> Now, what is the particular thing in Scripture, for the confirmation of which the indefectible authority of Scripture is thus invoked? It is one of its most casual clauses—more than that, the very form of its expression in one of its most casual clauses. This means, of course, that in the Saviour's view the indefectible authority of Scripture attaches to the very form of expression of its most casual clauses. It belongs to Scripture through and through, down to its most minute particulars, that it is of indefectible authority.[41]

In the second place, the essence of our Lord's argument depends on *one word:* "gods." The authority of Scripture attaches to a single word in a casual clause. If found in the "Law," it is authoritative, and the authority extends to a single word in the Law. Is this not what is meant by verbal-plenary inspiration?

Speaking about fifteen years ago at Dallas Theological Seminary, Edward J. Young, late professor of Old Testament at Westminster Theological Seminary, referred to the words "and the Scripture cannot be broken," calling them "a brief summary of the Protestant position on Scripture."[42]

3. A third truth appears from the conversation with the Jews. Jesus had spoken to them of the absolute unity that existed between the Father and Himself (v. 30). They evidently thought this claim to be a claim to deity (v. 33). And with His words in verse 36 He acknowledges that He is the Son of God.[43] He does not say that He is *making Himself* the Son of God, as they thought. He is not *making Himself* anything at all. He *is* the Son of God. And it is clear from verse 33 that the Jews understood this to be a claim to deity. The theism of Judaism always tended to a theanthropism, to a real and final union of God and man, and Jesus found it typified in the calling of the ancient judges by the name of "gods." In the final analysis it had to be this, for otherwise there could be no true revelation of God and no valid atonement.

The claim of our Lord throws into sharp contrast the heterodox denial of the deity of the Son. It is absurd to claim to be a Christian and deny His full deity. If He was not the Son of God, as He claimed, then His death was not a glorious satisfaction for our sins, but a wholly deserved end for a blasphemer. If He was not the Son of God, then His trial and condemnation were just, and His execution by crucifixion was one of the most righteous acts ever performed by human government. In fact, if He was not the Son of God, "very God of very God," then there is no reason whatever for a written New Testament. If He was not the Son of God, our preaching is vain, our faith is vain, and we are still in our sins. If Christ was not God, then we are of all men most miserable. But since He is God, coequal and coeternal with the Father, then all that He claimed is true and all that

He accomplished is truly ours: His saving death and resurrection, the forgiveness of our sins, and our hope of eternal life. If there is no folly like the folly of denying His sonship and deity, there is also no joy like the assurance of it.

CONCLUSION

We conclude this chapter with a deep sense of the full authority and inspiration of Holy Scripture and with the strong consolation that comes from the realization that the promises of God are, therefore, fully reliable. We have seen in this initial study that the phenomena of Scripture, in this case Jesus' resting His case on a single word in a casual clause, agree with the express statement "the Scripture cannot be broken."

We also note that the psalm to which He referred formed a solemn indictment and admonition directed to the judges of His day, to just such men as were standing before Him with stones in their hands, and to all who find it unendurable to acknowledge His majesty and sovereign grace. They may slay Him, but they must not forget that, according to the warning of the psalm, unjust judges "will die like men, and fall like any one of the princes" (Ps. 82:7).

3

1 Corinthians 9:7–10
The Question
of Pauline Hermeneutics

INTRODUCTION

A few years ago in a commencement address at one of our leading evangelical theological seminaries, the president of one of our leading evangelical colleges referred to Paul as a man "who got more out of the Old Testament Scriptures than the Holy Spirit put in them." The sentiment is not startling, since it is one held by many contemporary liberal students of the Bible. But coming from a conservative Christian college president, it was startling to me. It reflected the tremendous influence that liberal scholarship has gained among evangelicals.

The matter, however, points to something more serious. Is it possible to claim divine inspiration for writings that are manifest distortions of the texts they profess to cite in support of doctrinal teaching? Dewey Beegle thinks that it is possible to speak of the essential accuracy and trustworthiness of texts that deviate from the meaning they bore in their original setting. Just so long as the truth that is said to be found in them is "essential truth," it does not matter whether the sense claimed in the New Testament for an Old Testament text is really there. Beegle does not define his terms, but it is obvious even to a neophyte that he is operating with a different concept of truth from that of the Bible.

The illustration to which Beegle appeals in defense of his doctrine is Matthew's use of Hosea 11:1 in Matthew 2:14–15. It appears to him that Hosea's reference is one that points backward to the Exodus, and not forward to the time of our Lord and the departure of Joseph, Mary, and the child for Egypt. "There is not the slightest hint that the statement was intended as a prophecy," he claims.[1] That comment raises another question—which will be discussed later—namely, whether it was necessary for a prophet to understand everything that he wrote under the inspiration of the Spirit. Beegle goes on to say that Matthew's use of Hosea 11:1 is an unintentional distortion of the Old Testament passsage. How can he be sure it was unintentional? We are to conclude from this "phenomenon" that we cannot accept the inerrancy of Scripture. Matthew has departed from "absolute truth" in his handling of the Word of God, thus revealing that his own concept of Scripture is not that of inerrancy.[2]

This is not the time to deal with the passage in Matthew 2:14–15, but I would like to ask Beegle one simple question: "Is typology not a valid aspect of biblical interpretation and a common feature of the relation of the Old Testament to the New Testament, and are not many of the antitypical realities called 'fulfillments' in the New Testament?" Whether Hosea understood the full significance of his words or not we will probably never know, but we do know that the Holy Spirit intended by them to relate the Egypt event of the Old Testament to the Egypt event of the New. He has made that known to us by the hand of the evangelist.[3] Beegle would call Matthew's use of the Old Testament an illustration of how "erroneous nonessentials" do not invalidate essential truth. In this case, however, what is the essential truth that is left after Matthew's bungling of the text? A superfluous excess of torturing a text!

We have a similar situation in the Pauline handling of Deuteronomy 25:4 in 1 Corinthians 9:7–10. Of the apostle's exegesis James Moffatt comments deprecatingly:

For Paul, the literal sense of the injunction had no significance at all; it is one drawback of mystical or allegorical interpretations that, in extracting what is supposed to be the higher meaning of a text or incident, they often miss the profound, direct, significance of the literal statement.[4]

In his more recent work C. K. Barrett, who stands in the front rank of today's New Testament interpreters, has followed the same line of interpretation:

Attempts to show that Paul did not mean that God did not care about the animals break down on the next clause: *Or is he not speaking simply (πάντως) on our account?* The only interpretation that is not forced is that in the Old Testament law God had in mind not oxen, but Christian preachers and their needs. This does not mean that Paul would have denied the truth (quoted here by Calvin; see also Barth, C.D. III. iii. 174) that God is concerned even over the fall of a sparrow; but it was a quite different truth that he found in the Old Testament and expressed here. His argument is not of the *a minori ad maius (qal wahomer)* kind to which there are rabbinic parallels (S.B. iii. 385): God cares for oxen, therefore so much more for men (Weiss).[5]

If Moffatt and Barrett are correct, we must admit that the phenomena of the Bible, in this case the use of the Old Testament in the New, give us a different theory of inspiration than the traditional view. It cannot be said that the inspiration the Bible teaches is of the verbal-plenary mold if the apostle erroneously handles the Scriptures.

We would, then, be justified in ridiculing the methods of the apostles, just as, in fact, do many professors in our theological institutions. A few years ago, while on a sabbatical from the institution in which I was teaching, I attended classes in dogmatics at the University of Edinburgh, Scotland. A professor in one class made the point that the patristic authors continued and systematized what was begun in the Bible. He made two claims: (1) Their minds were "blown" by the resurrection and, because of that, they looked back to the preresurrected Jesus. They sought to learn under the Spirit's teaching, as He had promised in John 14 and 16. (2) They were forced to look again at the Old Testament. They interpreted the resurrection by the Old Testament and then they interpreted the Old Testament by the New Testament. It was not long before the Fathers saw much in the first words of Genesis (cf. 2 Cor. 4:3–6). Then the professor added, "You'll get fed up with the way the Fathers treat the Old Testament, and you'll get fed up with the way Paul does, too. Take the incident of 1 Corinthians 9. Paul talks there about the oxen and other things. That was rather naughty of Paul!"[6] We shall see who was "naughty," Paul or the professor.

There is another question raised by this passage, and it is not an unimportant question. In fact, we may turn it into a question with three related parts. First, do passages of Scripture often have more than one meaning? Second, is the work of the biblical interpreter finished when he has come to the meaning intended by the original human author? And, finally, if we are able to establish the principle that the Old Testament, for example, may contain meanings beyond the ken of the original human author, are *we* justified in practicing this principle in our study of other parts of the Old Testament? These are some of the aspects of the present study to which we will give attention at a later point. In the meantime let us turn to 1 Corinthians 9:7–10 for an investigation of Paul's hermeneutics in the light of biblical inspiration.

The New Testament Context of 1 Corinthians 9:7–10

This passage is found in the section of 1 Corinthians that deals with things sacrificed to idols (cf. 8:1–11:1). *Principles* are set forth in chapter 8. In chapter 9 Paul turns to the *illustration* of the principles. In spite of what some commentators have supposed, there is no divergence from the general theme. Rather, Paul illustrates the principle of sacrificing liberty for the sake of love, the point of chapter 8, by an appeal to his own experience. As an apostle and one who also possessed Christian liberty, he could claim financial support from those to whom he preached (9:1–14). Actually, however, he refused to exercise his rights in order to gain a reward (9:15–23). Such a decision demanded personal discipline and privation (9:24–27). The Corinthians, of course, were to apply the lesson of self-denial and discipline to the problem of meat sacrificed to idols.

In the immediate context of the citation from the Old Testament the apostle, after settling the matter of apostleship (vv. 1–4), argues his right to support, which derived from the apostolic gift (vv. 5–14). The first ground is the example of others (vv. 5–6), and the second is the principle of common right (v. 7). The third ground is the teaching of the Scriptures (vv. 8–10).

In establishing the third ground, Paul appeals to Deuteronomy, bringing us to the setting of our text from the Old Testament. The opening clause of verse 8 is paraphrased by Moffatt, "Oh, you may say, but these are secular, *human arguments.* What Scripture have you for your plea?"[7] The words ὁ νόμος ("the Law") seem to be used in the sense of "Scripture," although the citation is from Deuteronomy 25:4 (cf. 1 Cor. 14:21).

The γὰρ ("for") of verse 9 introduces the justification from the Mosaic section of the Scriptures, "You shall not muzzle an ox while he is threshing." Quickly Paul follows with a question expecting a negative answer, "God is not concerned about oxen, is He?" Moffatt's paraphrase is this: "You may object, 'But what has this to do with Christian apostles?' Everything! As if *God was thinking about cattle* when he laid down this rule *in the law of Moses!*"[8] Now, we must be careful here, for at first glance it appears that Paul says that God does not care for His own creation, making Moffatt right in his contention that for Paul the literal sense of the passage has no significance at all. We shall speak to the point in a moment, but it is sufficient here to refer to the comments of one of the older scholars: "When Paul asks if God *takes care for oxen,* it is clear that he is not speaking of God as Creator, but of God as giving the law (ver. 8), *in ferenda lege,* as Calvin says; for in the domain of creation and Providence 'He does not neglect even the smallest sparrow' (Calvin)."[9] The word ἐγράφη ("it was written") in verse 10 supports this conclusion.

The meaning of the disjunctive ἢ ("or") in verse 10 is this: *Or,* if He has not said λέγει ["is He speaking"]; cf. λαλῶ , v. 8 ["I am speaking"]) this for the sake of oxen, *does He for our sakes assuredly say it?* The πάντως is difficult, but it may mean "purely"[10] or "entirely," but also "certainly" or "surely" (cf. Luke 4:23). I like this latter meaning here.[11] The γὰρ (NASB "yes") that follows has a sense it sometimes has when it implies an affirmative answer to a previous question (cf. 1 Thess. 2:20). It means "yea" or, better, "yes indeed." The ὅτι following ("because") may mean "that" ("to show that,"[12] or declarative), or "because." The Authorized Version has "that." The δι᾽ ἡμᾶς ("for our sake") does not, as almost all assume, refer in Paul's mind directly to the apostles. If this were true, we should have expected ὑπὲρ ἡμῶν, "on our behalf." As Godet, in contrast to Barrett in the introduction, writes:

> The opposite of oxen is men, and not apostles. Paul does not, therefore, in the least suppress the historical and natural meaning of the precept, as is thought by de Wette, Ruckert, Meyer, Reuss, Edwards, and so many others. He recognizes it fully, and it is precisely by starting from this sense that he rises to a higher application. In the conduct which God prescribes to man toward this animal, which serves him as a faithful worker, Paul finds the proof of the conduct which man should with stronger reason observe toward his human servants, and with still stronger reason the Church toward its ministers. This entire gradation would crumble instantly were the lowest step of the scale suppressed, that which was directly present to the mind of Moses; a fact which was understood by the apostle as well as by those who criticize him. Far from arbitrarily allegorizing, he applies, by a well-rounded *a fortiori,* to a higher relation what God has prescribed witn reference to a lower relation.[13]

THE OLD TESTAMENT CONTEXT OF DEUTERONOMY 25:4

The Old Testament passage is found in the section of Deuteronomy in which various covenant stipulations are being set forth (cf. 12:1–26:19). The immediate context has to do with a number of social laws, such as exemption from military service (cf. 24:5), the taking of millstones in pledge (v. 6), kidnapping of a person (v. 7), leprosy (vv. 8–9), loans (vv. 10–13), protection for hired servants (vv. 14–15), personal responsibility (v. 16), protection of the weak and defenseless (vv. 17–18), the law of gleaning (vv. 19–22), and the limits of corporal punishment (25:1–3). It is plain that the commands are directed toward the inculcation of care and consideration toward the poor, the weak, and the defenseless. The Israelite was to restore at sundown a garment as a pledge from a poor man in a loan (cf. 24:10–13). The poor laborer was to be paid his wages every evening (vv. 14–15). The child must not be put to death with a guilty father (vv. 16–18). A gleaning for widows and strangers was to be left in the fields when the harvest was being gathered in (vv. 19–22). And a criminal was not to be subjected to more than forty stripes—a figure also found in the Assyrian Code (25:1–3; cf. 2 Cor. 11:24).[14]

At this point 25:4 follows: "You shall not muzzle the ox while he is threshing." It is important to note, too, that immediately after the reference to the "ox" Moses continues to speak of "people." There are several things to be noted here.

1. The series of injunctions in the context is designed to inculcate in the hearts of God's people a sense of *moral justice and equity.* The laws surrounding Deuteronomy 25:4 indicate that this was the chief force of that text, too. As Godet says:

> It was not from solicitude for oxen that God made this prohibition [I would only add to Godet's words the word *only* after "not"]; there were other ways of providing for the nourishment of these animals. By calling on the Israelites to exercise gentleness and gratitude, even toward a poor animal, it is clear that God desired to inculcate on them, with stronger reason, the same way of acting toward the human workmen whose help they engaged in their labour. It was the duties of *moral* beings to one another, that God wished to impress by this precept.[15]

2. There is another approach to the text in Deuteronomy that has been suggested by some. Since the text is about animals in a general context dealing with people and since it does lend itself to classification as a proverbial statement (its use in the New Testament may suggest this; cf. 1 Tim. 5:18), it is not at all certain to some students that it was not used figuratively from the very first.[16] The practice of leaving unmuzzled animals treading out corn still prevails among Eastern peoples.[17] The Law-giver may have been alluding to a proverb, which came to be applied to men as well as animals. If this could be demonstrated, a different view of the passage would emerge.

Some years ago, when teaching on the subject of this particular citation from the Old Testament, I commented that the text's proverbial character may be supported by the fact that Paul cited it twice in his writing. One of my students facetiously asked, "Was this Paul's 'life verse,' then?" In an outburst of uncommon sharpness, I replied, "No, but perhaps it was the life verse of the oxen!"

THE COMPARISON OF THE OLD AND NEW TESTAMENT TEXTS

Again, for purposes of comparison the relevant Old and New Testament texts are set forth below.

NT	LXX	MT
(1 Cor. 9:9)	(Deut. 25:4)	(Deut. 25:4)
IF: ἐν γὰρ τῷ Μωϋσέως νόμῳ γέγραπται·		
οὐ κημώσεις βοῦν ἀλοῶντα.	οὐ φιμώσεις βοῦν ἀλοῶντα.	לֹא־תַחְסֹם שׁוֹר בְּדִישׁוֹ׃

Targum
(Deut. 25:4)

לָא־תַחֵיד פּוּם־תּוֹרָא בִּדְיָשֵׁיה׃

IF: For it is written in the Law of Moses,

"You shall not muzzle the ox while he is threshing."	You shall not muzzle the ox while he is threshing.	You shall not muzzle the mouth of the ox while he is threshing.

You shall not muzzle the ox while he is threshing [lit., "in his threshing"].

COMMENTS ON VARIATIONS IN THE TEXTS

It is difficult to be certain of the reading in the New Testament. The verb φιμώσεις has perhaps the better attestation externally, but it is hard to see how κημώσεις arose, if the former, the more literary word, was genuine. In 1 Timothy 5:18 φιμώσεις is genuine. Further, since κημόω is the rarer word, the tendency of scribes would be to correct it to the more common word, which also happens to be the reading of the LXX, another reason for correction. Thus, both external and internal considerations suggest preference for κημώσεις .[18] Chrysostom and Theodoret also support it. Fortunately, the two verbs mean the same thing. In this case Paul seems to have translated from the Hebrew or Aramaic.

PAUL'S HERMENEUTICAL USE OF THE OLD TESTAMENT

The chief problem of the passage has to do with the Pauline hermeneutics and its bearing on the doctrine of biblical inspiration. Moffatt has stated flatly, and Barrett follows him, that for Paul the literal sense had no significance at all. The former commentator thinks that he uses allegory, or follows a spiritual interpretation, similar to Philo's or that of the Epistle of Aristeas.[19] Is this true?

Perhaps this is a little strong, but the position of Moffatt reminds me of another British scholar's comments concerning a particular theory of successive recensions and redactions of Matthew's Gospel. He referred to the theory as "a mere pile of unjustifiable conjectures that totters the moment it is touched, and tumbles the moment it is touched again."[20] Lord Bacon authored an aphorism regarding the interpretation of legal documents that bears directly on the interpretation of the biblical records as well, "Interpretation that departs from the letter of the text is not interpretation but divination." Let us bear this in mind as we look at Paul's usage.

1. The older commentators tend to the view that Paul was not dismissing the literal meaning.[21] A lot depends on the force given the πάντως (NASB "altogether"; NIV "surely"). With negatives the adverb may have the meaning of "not at all," a meaning that would support the idea that Paul was concerned only about the application of the text to human beings (cf. 1 Cor. 16:12; Rom. 3:9). On the other

hand, without negatives it has a strong affirmative force, such as "by all means," "certainly," "probably," "doubtless" (cf. Luke 4:23; Acts 28:4).[22] "At least" has been suggested for 1 Corinthians 9:22.[23] Barrett has "simply" in verse 10, but "at all events" in verse 22. Arndt and Gingrich suggest the rendering for the clause, "or is he (not) certainly speaking in our interest?"[24] Since the clause does have the nuance of a strong affirmation, the sense of "surely" fits well. Then the following clause follows naturally, "Yes, indeed [γὰρ],[25] for our sake it was written."

Thus the apostle acknowledges that the Old Testament text, while not exclusively for men, does have an application to them. The literal meaning is not excluded, but the text is given a further spiritual or moral sense. In one sense, the passage is seen as referring to God, not as *the* Creator who cares for His creation (cf. Ps. 104:14, 21, 27; 145:9, 15; Matt. 6:26; 10:30), but as the Law-giver. As such it had a significance beyond the oxen, namely, that of moral justice to men. This viewpoint is in harmony with the apostle's words in 1 Corinthians 10:6, 11.

Luther, in his characteristic way, said the passage was not for oxen, because oxen cannot read!

2. In the rabbinic literature Deuteronomy 25:4 was often used "as a sort of norm for the elucidation of other texts; it was very freely applied in an analogical sense, though no rabbi suggests that the literal meaning can be ignored."[26] It is possible that by the time of the writing of 1 Timothy 5:18 the text had become one used primarily in a practical sense, that is, in application.

If, as is possible, the saying was from the beginning proverbial in nature, as Keil appears to take it, then the passage in 1 Corinthians is clear. The statement from the Old Testament, while a literal one in its original context, had primary reference to the moral principle behind it—justice and equity. The apostles, Keil believes, understood it in this way. It seems clear, then, that there is no justification for thinking that Paul has misused the Old Testament text.[27]

To sum up, it is likely that Paul has used the Old Testament passage analogically, although the proverbial use may not be completely ruled out. There is no evidence that the literal sense of the Old Testament text was of no significance for Paul.

PAUL'S THEOLOGICAL USE OF THE OLD TESTAMENT

There are several conclusions of theological significance that emerge from the apostle's handling of Scripture in this passage.

1. It is important to notice that Paul's words in verse 9 clearly point to his conviction that the Law of Moses is really the voice of God. The Law is the "Law of Moses," nevertheless the words are the words of God, for he adds, "God is not concerned about oxen, is He?" thus making it plain that the text was really from God. Thus what we have here, as elsewhere throughout the Bible, is the double authorship of Scripture, with God the source of the Word and man the means by which it comes to us.

Again, we note that in the final analysis the phenomena of Scripture support the divine authorship of Scripture. The Word is the Word *of God.* Implicit throughout the Old Testament is that "All Scripture is God-breathed" (cf. 2 Tim. 3:16), that is, God is the source of revealed truth. Words that in the Old Testament referred to the human authors are referred to God in the New (cf. Matt. 19:4–5 [cf. Gen. 2:24]; Heb. 1:6 [cf. Deut. 32:43]; Heb. 2:13 [cf. Isa. 8:17–18]; Heb. 4:4; 10:30 [cf. Deut. 32:36]). This can be done only on the hypothesis that all Scripture is really a declaration of God.[28]

2. It is also clear from this use of the Old Testament in the New that there may exist more than one sense in the same Scripture. Passages written of specific historical situations may indeed express principles that pertain to other situations also. And this is apart from the whole subject of typology and prophecy in their various forms. Whether we call this "extended significance"[29] or not, it does seem true to the interpretation of these passages to affirm that many texts have a meaning that goes beyond their normal historical sense, valid though that surely is.

3. A third question may be raised at this point: Is it proper to say that a passage of Scripture may possess meanings in addition to that which was known by the original human author? Put in another

way, is the interpreter's work concluded when he has arrived at the meaning intended by the human author?

E. D. Hirsch, Jr. of the University of Virginia a few years ago wrote a book of great importance for interpretation. Hirsch's work, entitled *Validity in Interpretation* and written in the context of the debate over the new hermeneutics in the writings of Fuchs, Ebeling, Gadamer, Betti, and others, has sought to demonstrate that the key aim of the interpreter is to find "the author's willed meaning."[30] Hermeneutics for Hirsch is simply the logic of validation of the author's will, which is changeless, reproducible, and determinate.[31] One must distinguish between verbal meaning and significance (the meaning for us today). Verbal meaning is the goal of hermeneutics.

We may agree with Hirsch, providing that it is understood that the "authorial will" we are seeking as interpreters is God's intended sense. Hirsch grants that.[32] It would seem, then, that in interpreting a text we should not be surprised to find that the authorial will of God goes beyond the human authorial will, particularly in those sections of the Word of God that belong to the earlier states in the historical process of special revelation, that is, in the Old Testament.

Packer, while agreeing with this conclusion, adds a stricture that is important:

> If, as in one sense is invariably the case, God's meaning and message through each passage, when set in its total biblical context, exceeds what the human writer had in mind, that further meaning is only an extension and development of his, a drawing out of implications and an establishing of relationships between his words and other, perhaps later, biblical declarations in a way that the writer himself, in the nature of the case, could not do. Think, for example, how messianic prophecy is declared to have been fulfilled in the New Testament, or how the sacrificial system of Leviticus is explained as typical in Hebrews. The point here is that the *sensus plenior* which texts acquire in their wider biblical context remains an extrapolation on the grammatico-historical plane, not a new projection onto the plane of allegory. And, though God may have more to say to us from each text than its human author had in mind, God's meaning is never less than his. What he means, God means.[33]

In connection with this, quite often interpreters of the Old Testament complain that this constitutes a "reading of New Testament truth back into the Old Testament," and this we are not to do. Of course, we should always interpret the Old Testament text in its grammatico-historico-spiritual sense initially. But to use this as an excuse to reject typical and prophetic sense in Scripture is, à la Hirsch, to reject authorial will, as the use of the Old Testament in the New Testament indicates.

In Donald Miller's words, "Thus the approach to the Old Testament for purely historical purposes, and the approach to it for the purposes of Christian theology, are both valid—but the latter must finally command the former."[34]

CONCLUSION

We conclude, then, that the apostle Paul did not get more out of the Old Testament Scriptures than the Holy Spirit put into them. Further, we find after careful study of the apostles' writings that we do not find their handling of the Word of God to be "rather naughty."

Paul found a valid moral sense in the passage from Deuteronomy 25:4 and, although he stressed this sense of the text, it was really there! It is only the careless student who fails to see it, too.

Thus the work of the biblical interpreter is not necessarily finished when he has come to the meaning intended by the original human author. Payne is right when he said, "Intention should guide exegesis only tentatively and as the text opens it up. Ultimately the *text* is the source from which the exegete draws meaning."[35] The total context of a passage is necessary for its correct understanding and, therefore, the intention of the secondary author must be subordinated to the intention of the primary author, God Himself. The biblical principle of the *analogia Scripturae* should have taught us that. *Scriptura ex Scriptura explicanda est,* or *Scriptura sui ipsius interpres,* traditional expressions of the sense of the analogy, teach that our first and final task is to discern God's intention in the text of Scripture. After all, is not the Bible *God's* Word?

Hebrews 10:5-7
The Place of
Typology in Exegesis

INTRODUCTION

The New Testament book that surpasses all the others in its direct and indirect use of the Old Testament is the anonymous Epistle to the Hebrews.[1] It is therefore unnecessary to stress the significance of the Old Testament for the understanding of the book. The argument of the letter is, in fact, built on four great prophetic utterances from the Old Testament, the first two of which are closely related and perhaps belong together. These four utterances are:

1 and 2. Psalm 2 and Psalm 110, which teach that there is to be a *new priesthood,* grounded in a Son who is the messianic King. The two psalms are very closely related in the author's thinking, as is evident from his use of them (cf. Heb. 1:5, 13; 5:5, 6; 7:11-19, 20-25, 28). He argues that sonship is necessary if a priesthood is to have an eternal character. Only an eternal Son of God can really be an eternal priest of God. The two texts serve to support this thesis.

3. Jeremiah 31:31-34, which describes a *new covenant.*

4. Psalm 40:7-9, which enunciates a *new sacrifice.*

Actually, all the prophetic utterances demonstrate the high

priesthood of Jesus Christ. This is the author's primary theme, as is seen by his statement in 8:1 (Gr. $\kappa\epsilon\phi\acute{a}\lambda\alpha\iota\sigma\nu$ $\delta\grave{\epsilon}$ $\grave{\epsilon}\pi\grave{\iota}$ $\tauο\hatio\varsigma$ $\lambda\epsilon$-$\gamma\sigma\mu\acute{\epsilon}\nuο\iota\varsigma$; NIV "the point of what we are saying").[2]

There are several facts to be aware of as we continue to analyze the ways the Old Testament is used in the New. In the first place, contrary to our modern practice of precise documentation, *exact, verbatim citation* was not common in the Graeco-Roman world of the first century A.D.[3] Direct discourse was occasionally indicated by a recitative $\acute{ο}\tau\iota$, but this marked only the beginning of a citation, not its end.[4] The meaning of the passage was the important thing. "Odd as it may seem to us," Manson pointed out, "the freedom with which they handled the Biblical text is a direct result of the supreme importance which they attached to it."[5] Memory citation, thus, was quite common.[6]

Second, it is possible to discover the text that served as the writer's source for the citations from the Old Testament. There are three principal possibilities:

1. A Hebrew text, either non-Masoretic or proto-Masoretic (the Hebrew text of the first century A.D., so called inasmuch as it resembles the later text).

2. A Greek text from the Septuagint tradition, or one parallel to that tradition.

3. An Aramaic Targum text (whether oral or written), reflecting the interpretive, paraphrastic translations in use during the New Testament period.

As materials for criticism we now have:

1. The standard Masoretic text and portions of the Hebrew text from Qumran, both in proto-Masoretic form and in Septuagint form.

2. The Septuagint manuscripts, from the fourth century A.D. in complete form. The Septuagint is important for New Testament interpretation because of the ways the New Testament authors used it. A famous German scholar, Hitzig, once said to his students, *"Meine Herren, haben Sie eine Septuaginta? Wenn nicht, so verkaufen Sie alles was Sie haben, und kaufen sich eine Septuaginta!"*[7]

3. Manuscripts of the Targums of the Pentateuch and the Prophets, dating from the fifteenth and sixteenth centuries in complete

form, but attested to in various ways in the Middle Ages and earlier.[8]

Typology is closely connected to the question of the relationship between the use of the Old Testament in the New and the biblical doctrine of inspiration.[9] The failure to understand biblical typology often accounts for the inability to appreciate the validity of the ways the Old Testament is used in the New Testament. For example, Beegle contends that Matthew's use of Hosea 11:1 in Matthew 2:14–15 is invalid. Matthew says that the text from Hosea 11:1, "Out of Egypt have I called my son," a clear reference to the exodus of Israel from Egypt under Moses, is "fulfilled" by the return of the young Jesus from Egypt to Nazareth after the death of Herod. Beegle thinks he has demonstrated the error in Matthew's hermeneutics by commenting, "The sense of the passage and the intention of the prophet point backward, not forward. There is not the slightest hint that the statement was intended as a prophecy."[10] Beegle has failed to appreciate Matthew's use of typology and his understanding of the term "fulfilled."

It is sufficient at this point to note that Matthew's usage is a typical one. The nation's return from Egypt corresponds to Jesus' return from Egypt. The relationship is even closer, for, as Gundry points out, "Jesus is the representative Israelite in whose individual history the history of the whole nation, apart from its sin and apostasy, is recapitulated and anticipated."[11]

Enough has been said to indicate that Matthew's use of the Old Testament is not errant at all. Through a skillful use of typology the author displays a deep sense of the christological, unified *Heilsgeschichte,* (salvation history) found in the Bible. Westcott put it succinctly: "A type presupposes a purpose in history wrought out from age to age."[12]

Many years ago R. W. Dale defined a type as "the exhibition, in an inferior form, of a truth, a principle, a law, which is revealed in a higher form in the Christian dispensation."[13] Although Dale's definition has in it many of the essentials of typology, it needs to be expanded. Typology is the study of the spiritual correspondences between persons, events, and things within the historical framework of God's special revelation. Woollcombe's definition is similar:

Typology, considered as a method of exegesis, may be defined as the establishment of historical connexions between certain events, persons or things in the Old Testament and similar events, persons or things in the New Testament. Considered as a method of writing, it may be defined as the description of an event, person or thing in the New Testament in terms borrowed from the description of its prototypal counterpart in the Old Testament.[14]

The principal features of typology, according to these definitions, are the ideas of correspondence, historicity, and predictiveness. It is the conviction of some that predictiveness does not really belong to a type, for in the type itself there is no "intrinsic reference" to the future, or the future age.[15] France, for example, holds that the human author of the type did not generally intend that the type be predictive. That the human author did not usually so intend or understand the forward-looking features of his writing may be granted. But Scripture is a divine as well as a human product; God is the source and man only the agent in its communication. In the sense that Scripture ultimately comes from God, His intention that the Old Testament revelation should look forward to the New must be acknowledged. In this sense, then, we assert that predictiveness is an essential feature of a type. Further, the very use of the term "fulfilled," so common in the introduction of the antitypical in the New Testament, justifies our conclusion about the predictiveness of types.

The fundamental basis of typology is theological. Biblical typology is built squarely on *the sovereignty of God.* It is He who controls history and, therefore, guides events in such a way that types find their correspondence in antitypes. Typology is also built on *the immutability of God.* God works in history according to the unchanging nature of His being. The repetition of the acts of God through history point to a consistency in divine dealings with men. The Exodus from Egypt will be followed by a future Exodus on a grander scale (cf. Isa. 11:10–16; Jer. 23:1–8). We might also add that typology is based on *the wisdom of God* as well, for the entire material is a grand display of the infinite wisdom of our Triune God working out the unified purpose of the ages (cf. Eph. 3:11).[16]

In all that we have said concerning typology, however, we are not ignoring the eisegesis that has been offered in the name of typology. Our teachers in typology usually begin by stressing misuse and overemphasis in understanding biblical types. For example, Mickelsen warns, "No area of biblical interpretation needs more careful definition than typology."[17] This warning arises out of a use of typology that many people regard as extreme. Extreme typological interpretation has been with us for a long time. For example, the "two wings of the great eagle" of Revelation 12:13 are probably not the U. S. Air Force nor our Phantom Jets! Further, Ezekiel's vision of the living creatures and wheels probably does not refer to UFOs operated by the cherubim, as a radio preacher suggested a few years ago. The many wives of Solomon are not a typical representation of the many virtues of his character, nor is Samson's meeting of the young lion a type of Christ's encounter with Saul on the Damascus road. When Jacob purchased Esau's birthright with red pottage, there is no reference to Christ's purchase of heaven for His people by His red blood. Jacob's being clothed with Esau's garment when the blessing was stolen does not picture Christ's being clothed with our nature when the purchase was consummated.[18]

This bizarre kind of exegesis must be wholeheartedly rejected. An attempt to find the political squabbles and denominational battles of the twentieth century in the Old Testament is a risky undertaking at best.

Yet in our fear of overdoing typology we must not succumb to the biting, rationalistic ridicule of those who denigrate typology. We may then be guilty of ignoring what God has stressed. One of the happier results of twentieth-century biblical scholarship has been the rediscovery of the importance of typology for the understanding of the Bible. I am hopeful that evangelicals, who so often follow rather than lead in biblical scholarship, will follow once again, for in this case modern scholarship is surely right.

My aim in this chapter will be, first, to take an overall look at the context of the quotation of Psalm 40 in Hebrews 10:5–7, treating synthetically 9:1–10:18; then to look at the author's exegesis of the passage from the Psalms; and finally to offer a few observations on his use of the Old Testament.

THE GENERAL CONTEXT OF THE NEW SACRIFICE PASSAGE

In Hebrews 2:17 the author first mentions the high priesthood of Christ, but it is not until 4:14 that his discussion begins in earnest. After outlining the qualifications for priesthood (5:1–10), the validity of the new priesthood (7:1–28), which serves within a new covenant (8:1–13), the author launches into a lengthy discussion of the once-for-all sacrifice that establishes the new covenant and the new priesthood forever (9:1–10:18).

The steps in this last argument need to be discussed more fully.

The old covenant sanctuary and service (9:1–10)

Using the annual service of the Day of Atonement as the backdrop, the author of Hebrews briefly describes the tabernacle and its furniture. It is significant that he concentrates on the tabernacle rather than on the temple. He is writing for Christians who are on the way to the heavenly Jerusalem and have no continuing city on earth. The tabernacle was designed for people on the move to the Promised Land. It is fitting, therefore, for him to note that the old covenant service contained within itself an evidence of its transitoriness and inadequacy (vv. 6–8).

The new covenant sanctuary and service (9:11–28)

After an incidental reference to the better sanctuary (vv. 1–12), the author launches into a long discussion of the better service of the new covenant (vv. 13–28). In the first two verses he mentions the *sphere* (heaven), the *work* (sacrifice), and the *aim* (eternal redemption) of the Messiah. The last three words of verse 12 are then expanded in verses 13-14, an explanation being offered for the eternity of His sacrifice. The argument is *a fortiori.* The phrase διὰ πνεύματος αἰωνίου ("through the eternal Spirit") is the climactic point. The anarthrous noun (cf. v. 8) refers to the inward spirit of Christ, His spiritual nature. This sacrifice is no *ordinance of the flesh* (cf. v. 10). He offered *Himself,* He offered Himself *spotless,* He offered Himself spotless through the "whole power of His deathless personality."[19] Its worth can never fade, for it is offered in the eternal order of spirit by a sinless personality who posessed the nature of eternity. Hallelujah! What a Savior!

In verses 15–22 the author turns logically ($\delta\iota\grave{\alpha}$ $\tau o\hat{v}\tau o$; "for this reason") to the covenant that was established by this sacrifice. He is at pains to show that the shedding of blood is essential to the covenant. We will not go into detail about the meaning of $\delta\iota\alpha\theta\acute{\eta}\kappa\eta$ (AV "testament"). In my opinion it is not clearly used in the New Testament in any place in the sense of "testament," or "testamentary disposition." Its usual meaning is "covenant." Adolf Deissmann attempted to force the meaning of "testament" on the word throughout the New Testament.[20] The word means "covenant" (cf. v. 18; note also the particles in vv. 16, 17, 18, 19—all connected to a statement about a "covenant" in v. 15; 7:22 [no surety needed for a will]).

In verses 23-28, the famous passage with the three appearings (v. 26—the cross in view; v. 24—the session; v. 28—the Second Coming), the author infers ($o\hat{v}\nu$, "therefore") from the preceding statement about the necessity of the blood that the heavenly sanctuary had to be cleansed, too. And so the section pictures this sacrifice, a perfect one that needs no repetition.

The new covenant sacrifice (10:1–18)

Hebrews 10:1 carries on the argument of 9:26, after the parenthesis of 9:27–28.[21] The writer's $\gamma\grave{\alpha}\rho$ ("for") indicates the connection. The inefficacy of the Levitical cultus is demonstrated in four ways:

1. The insubstantial character of the Mosaic economy (see 8:5; 10:1, $\sigma\kappa\iota\acute{\alpha}\nu$ [AV "shadow"]).[22]

2. The repetitive character of the sacrifices (vv. 1–3; cf. 7:27; 9:25). Repetition conflicts with finality, according to the author.

3. The repetitive reminders of sin, the repetition pointing to the need for a final sacrifice (cf. vv. 1–3; 8:12; 10:17).

4. The insufficiency of animal sacrifices (v. 4). They lacked personality, volition, and rationality, being unable to say, "Lo, I have come to do thy will, O God." They were divinely instituted, but propaedeutic, pointing to "the seriousness of sin, the reality of the righteousness of God, and the necessity for atonement."[23]

The δίό of verse five ("therefore," AV "wherefore") introduces an inference from the ineffectiveness of the Levitical sacrifices. The psalmist expresses human ideals that the Messiah alone could realize and acknowledges the inadequacy of the animal sacrifices. The Messiah offers the rational self-surrender that they were intended to represent. Psalm 40:6-8 is quoted to show that the Messiah's coming with a conscious desire to do God's will in sacrifice has resulted in a final and efficacious offering for man.

Furthermore, the Messiah's present session demonstrates the efficacy of His work (vv. 11-14). The author of Hebrews returns to the thought of Psalm 110, so prominent in this epistle, and interprets the "sat down" of verse 12 as a fulfillment of the opening words of Psalm 110. This he contrasts with the "priestly tread-mill of sacrifice" performed by "the Levitical drudges."[24]

Finally, returning to Jeremiah 31:31, 34, the author supports the final, effective sacrifice by its issue: the forgiveness of sins.[25] Verse 18 says, "Now where there is forgiveness of these things, there is no longer any offering for sin." Westcott comments, "This is the last—the decisive—word of the argument."[26]

THE EXEGESIS OF PSALM 40:6-8 IN HEBREWS

We now look at the interesting citation of Psalm 40, considering it textually, hermeneutically, and theologically. Note that in the Masoretic text the verses are numbered 7 to 9. The relevant texts are as follows:[27]

NT	LXX	MT
(Heb. 10:5-7)	(Ps. 40:6-8)	(Ps. 40:7-9)

IF: Διὸ εἰσερχόμενος εἰς τὸν κόσμον λέγει·

NT	LXX	MT
θυσίαν καὶ προσφορὰν οὐκ ἠθέλησας, σῶμα δὲ κατηρτίσω μοι· [6]ὁλοκαυτώματα καὶ περὶ ἁμαρτίας. οὐκ εὐδόκησας.	θυσίαν καὶ προσφορὰν οὐκ ἠθέλησας, ὠτία δὲ κατηρτίσω μοι· ὁλοκαύτωμα καὶ περὶ ἁμαρτίας οὐκ ἤτησας.	זֶבַח וּמִנְחָה לֹא־חָפַצְתָּ אָזְנַיִם כָּרִיתָ לִּי עוֹלָה וַחֲטָאָה לֹא שָׁאָלְתָּ: [8]אָז אָמַרְתִּי הִנֵּה־בָאתִי בִּמְגִלַּת־סֵפֶר כָּתוּב עָלָי: [9]לַעֲשׂוֹת־רְצוֹנְךָ אֱלֹהַי

Hebrews 10:5–7

⁷τότε εἶπον· ἰδοὺ
ἥκω, ἐν κεφαλίδι
βιβλίου γέγραπται
περὶ ἐμοῦ, τοῦ
ποιῆσαι ὁ θεὸς τὸ
θέλημά σου.

IF: Therefore, when He
comes into the world,
He says,

Sacrifice and offering
thou hast not desired,
but a body thou hast
prepared for me;
⁶In whole burnt offer-
ings and sacrifices for
sin thou hast taken no
pleasure.
⁷Then I said, Behold, I
have come (in the roll
of the book it is written
of me) to do thy will, O
God.

⁷Τὸτε εἶπον ἰδοὺ
ἥκω ἐν κεφαλίδι
βιβλίου γέγραπται
περὶ ἐμοῦ·
⁸τοῦ ποιῆσαι
τὸ θέλημά σου,
ὁ θεός μου,
ἐβουλήθην καὶ
τὸν νόμον σον
ἐν μέσῳ τῆς
κοιλίας μου.

⁶Sacrifice and offering
thou hast not desired,
but ears thou hast
prepared for me;
Whole burnt offerings
and sacrifices for sin
thou hast not required.
⁷Then I said, Behold, I
have come (in the roll
of the book it is written
of me).
⁸To do thy will, my
God, I have purposed,
and thy law is in the
midst of my belly.

חָפַצְתִּי וְתוֹרָתְךָ
בְּתוֹךְ מֵעָי:

Targum
(Ps. 40:7)

פּוּרְקָנָךְ כְּוֵיתָא לִי
אוּדְנִין לַאֲצָתָא

⁷Sacrifice and meal-
offering thou hast not
desired; my ears thou
hast dug; Burnt offer-
ing and sin offering
thou hast not required.
⁸Then I said, Behold, I
come: in the roll of the
book it is written of
[prescribed for?] me.
⁹I delight to do thy will,
O my God, and thy law
is within my heart.

⁷Ears for hearing your
salvation you have
pierced for me.

Textual considerations

There are three changes in the New Testament text from the
Septuagint[A/B] that emphasize the purpose of Christ's coming.
First, Auctor uses εὐδόκησας ("hast taken pleasure," AV "hast had
pleasure") instead of ἤτησας (LXX[B]; lit. "required"), or ἐκζήτησας
(LXX[SA]; lit. "sought"). Cf. Psalm 50:18. The New Testament word is
an interpretation of the meaning of the Hebrew and the Septua-
gint.[28] See 9:19–20.
   Second, the omission of ἐβουλήθην (lit. "I have purposed")

61

makes τοῦ ποιῆσαι ("to do") dependent on ἥκω ("I have come," AV "I come"), so that "to do thy will" becomes the purpose of His coming.

Third, the emphasis on the doing of God's will is further strengthened by the removal of "thy will" to the end of the clause, an antithetical parallelism being formed with the words "thou hast not desired" (cf. v. 5). This emphasis on the doing of God's will is confirmed by the repetition of the last phrase in verse 9 and by the placing of "will" in the emphatic position in verse 10 (see below for the significance).

The greatest variation from the Hebrew text of the Old Testament is found in the reference to the preparation of a body for the Messiah. The important words are the following:

Hebrew: אָזְנַיִם כָּרִיתָ לִּי: "My ears thou hast dug."

LXX (Rahlfs): ὠτία δὲ κατηρτίσω μοι: "Ears thou hast prepared for me."

NT: σῶμα δὲ κατηρτίσω μοι: "A body thou hast prepared for me."

ὠτία Ga, σῶμα BSA; cf. Heb. 10:5.

The translators of the Septuagint may have had before them a text in Hebrew that had "body" instead of "ears," but there is no external evidence for such a reading.

It is also possible that σῶμα is a copyist's error that early became entrenched in the Septuagint. Let us assume for the moment that ὠτία, "ears," is genuine. It is plausible to account for the σῶμα, "body," by dittography of the final sigma of ἠθέλησας, which would then have been read with the following ὠτία. The TI may have been confused with an M, as below:

ΗΘΕΛΗΣΑΣΩΤΙΑ
ΗΘΕΛΗΣΑΣΩΜΑ

The only evidence for ὠτία is the Hexaplaric recension, one Old Latin manuscript, and two minuscules (142, 156) that have ὦτα δέ. The external testimony is, therefore, very weak. I think σῶμα is correct in the Septuagint and that the author of Hebrews had a text that contained σῶμα Assuming that it is the primitive reading, we cannot decide whether the LXX translator had another wording before him, or just loosely rendered the general meaning of the Hebrew (see below).

The rendering of כָּרִיתָ ("opened"; lit. "dug") by κατηρτίσω ("prepared") either represents a different Hebrew word from the Masoretic text or, most likely, is simply a free rendering. At any rate, there is no authority for any other reading in the Septuagint.

Hermeneutical considerations

We should begin with a word regarding the psalm. David evidently had experienced some singular deliverance from the jaws of death (see v. 1, "cry"; cf. vv. 1–5 ET). He naturally asks, "How can I express my gratitude? Shall it be by sacrifices? No, sacrifices are not the ultimate demand of God. He desires *me*. It is not oblation, but obedience that pleases Him" (cf. 1 Sam. 15:22). So, in the language of a servant, of an inferior to a superior, David speaks of coming to the Lord to do His will, as the Word prescribed for him. He speaks of delighting in God's will and of His Law being in his heart. But David can do God's will only "falteringly."[29] The words thus go beyond David to David's greater Son, on whose lips the words are uniquely and preeminently appropriate (cf. John 6:38; 4:34; 6:14; 11:27 with εἰσερχόμενος εἰς τὸν κόσμον).

The Old Testament psalm is, therefore, a typical psalm (cf. v. 12). It speaks of David's own experience, but the description goes beyond the Old Testament's "sweet singer of Israel" to his greater Son, who alone among men has loved God perfectly.

It was the view of C. S. Lewis in his suggestive little book on the Psalms that Psalm 40 was making a direct reference to Christ, even though in verse 12 the author writes, "My iniquities have overtaken me." In Lewis's mind the iniquities of the psalmist are those that Christ bore for sinners. In other words, the sins of the psalmist were imputed sins, not his own personal sins. That would solve the problem of how a psalm in which the author confesses sin could refer to Christ. But it runs afoul of another problem. Never does a New Testament writer nor our Lord ever apply an Old Testament passage to Him in which the writer confesses or deplores his sin.[30] It is simpler, then, to take the psalm as a typical psalm. It speaks of David the king as suffering some of the trials of the righteous, but the language goes beyond him to the preeminent Suffering Servant of Jehovah, the Lord Jesus.

It is often claimed that Hebrews misuses the psalm because σῶμα ("body") is not found in the Hebrew text. This claim is faulty. The important word for the author is not σῶμα. It is the clause "to do thy will" (the ultimate thing). A careful reading of vv. 8–10 convinces one of that. Further, the New Testament citation contains a change in the position of the words τὸ θέλημά σου ("thy will"). They are removed to the end of the citation, although in the Septuagint they stand at the beginning of the final verse.[31] It is clear that Auctor intends the emphasis to fall on the doing of God's will, not on the word "body."[32] He has not misused the psalm. The psalm speaks of Christ typically, and the author's emphasis on the words "doing the will of God," rather than the word "body," is true to the thought of the Old Testament passage.[33]

A great deal has been made over the difference between the Septuagint (and through the Septuagint, of course, the New Testament) and the Hebrew texts. After all, the New Testament, following the Septuagint, speaks of the preparation of a body, while the Hebrew text speaks of the opening of ears. At first glance the difference between the Hebrew and the Septuagint seems to be considerable. And it is, verbally. However, in the context the same general notion of an instrument of obedience is conveyed by the idea of the opened (lit. digged) ears and the fitted body. Delitzsch speaks of the New Testament rendering from the Septuagint as "an easier and more general rendering of the Hebrew כָּרִיתָ."[34] Calvin makes this comment:

> But the Apostle followed the Greek translators when he said, "A body hast thou prepared"; for in quoting these words the Apostles were not so scrupulous, provided they perverted not Scripture to their own purpose. We must always have a regard to the end for which they quote passages, for they are very careful as to the main object, so as not to turn Scripture to another meaning; but as to words and other things, which bear not on the subject in hand, they use great freedom.[35]

Others have suggested that this is an example of synecdoche, the use of a part for the whole—here the ears standing for the body. But Westcott has done as well as any in explaining the reading in Hebrews: "The rendering must therefore be considered to be a free interpretation of the original text. In this respect it extends and emphasizes the fundamental idea. The 'body' is the instrument for fulfilling the divine command, just as the 'ear' is the instrument for receiving it."[36] There is no serious problem with the use of the passage by the author.

IMPORTANT FEATURES OF THE AUTHOR'S THEOLOGICAL THINKING

Paul and Hebrews on the aim of the Law

Paul repeatedly emphasizes that one of the primary purposes of the Law was to reveal sin (cf. Rom. 3:20; 4:15; 7:7–12). It is interesting to see the author of Hebrews discovering the same thing in the Law, although he sees it from a different perspective. Reasoning from experience, he reaches Paul's conclusion. The sacrifices annually renew the people's consciousness of sins; therefore, they can never take away sin and, in fact, serve only to bring home to the conscience its guilt (cf. Heb. 10:1–4).[37]

The author of Hebrews and the sacrificial system

The author makes it clear that Jesus Christ did not come to do away with sacrifice. The Christ of the Psalm is not rejecting sacrifice in favor of something else. As James Denney said: "Christ did not come into the world to be a good man: it was not for this that a body was prepared for him. He came to be a great High Priest, and the body was prepared for him, that by the offering of it he might put sinful men for ever into the perfect religious relation to God."[38] He came, then, simply to substitute for animal sacrifices His own final and personal sacrifice (cf. 10:10).

The author of Hebrews and the interpretation of the psalm

The words of the psalm are seen to be Christ's. The psalm was probably composed to express David's feeling toward the end of his persecution by Saul, when the promised kingdom was now in near view.[39] David sees that only perfect self-devotion can really express proper gratitude and make atonement. Such a confession rises above his power of fulfillment, describing what Christ has done as the Son of Man, through whom man's ideal has been realized (cf. 2:5–9). As Westcott says, "Thus the words are rightly applied to Him."[40] The "He says" of verse 5 is in order.

CONCLUSION

First of all, it is clear from the citation of Psalm 40 in Hebrews 10 that exact, verbatim citation is not the practice of the New Testament authors. In fact, such a practice is impossible when the original material is in Hebrew and the citation is in Greek. It is the meaning derived from the Old Testament passage that is important. That meaning must be in the Old Testament passage, and it is always in the citations from the Old Testament in the New. In this case, the citation is not verbatim, but the meaning the author draws from the Old Testament text is really there, and it is that meaning that he uses in his New Testament argumentation. The doctrine of inerrancy does not demand exact, verbatim citation from the Old Testament. It merely requires that the meaning the New Testament author finds in the Old Testament and uses in the New is really in the Old Testament. In this case that is patently true.[41]

And, finally, we have noted that the acknowledgment of the existence of a full typology in Scripture is necessary to an understanding of the use of the Old Testament in the New and, as an ancillary matter, to an understanding of the biblical doctrine of inspiration. At first reading it may not appear that Psalm 40 is really a psalm about the Messiah to come, but in the light of the typological principles of correspondence, history, and prediction (from the divine viewpoint) it becomes clear that it is. The biblical authors grounded their understanding of Scripture on these principles and found no difficulty in finding Christ in the Old Testament. Of course, they had a good teacher who was versed in these matters. He admonished two early disciples, who reported His chiding instruction to the eleven and others: " 'O foolish men and slow of heart to believe in all that the prophets have spoken! Was it not necessary for the Christ to suffer these things and to enter into His glory?' And beginning with Moses and with all the prophets, He explained to them the things concerning Himself in all the Scriptures" (Luke 24:25–27; see also vv. 33–35).

Should we follow the apostles and Christ in their handling of Scripture? Some hesitate at this point, realizing that we are not inspired as they were. It is wise to hesitate and ponder the question deeply, and we shall do this ourselves more fully later. Suffice it to say at this point that if the apostles are reliable guides in biblical teaching, then they surely are reliable guides in the doctrine of interpretation, and we must follow them. One of the greatest theologians of the twentieth century said concerning inspiration:

> We believe this doctrine of the plenary inspiration of the Scriptures primarily because it is the doctrine which Christ and his apostles believed, and which they have taught us. It may sometimes seem difficult to take our stand frankly by the side of Christ and his apostles. It will always be found safe.[42]

The sentiments apply just as aptly to the doctrine of interpretation.

5

John 13:18
The Place of
Typology in Exegesis

INTRODUCTION

As we saw in the preceding chapter, the language of Hebrews is the language of "God's kindergarten." It explains the typology of the Pentateuch. The author felt that the weakness of his readers was related to their ignorance of "the elementary principles of the oracles of God" (cf. Heb. 5:12). While he included within the words the messianic promises and other fundamental Old Testament doctrines (cf. 6:1–2), he felt his readers needed also the typical and antitypical truth of the divine revelation, particularly that of Aaron and Melchizedek, and of the priesthood and the services.

We have passed through a stage of the neglect of typology in biblical theology. Hengstenberg said many years ago that the "elucidation of the doctrine of types, now entirely neglected, is an important problem for future theologians."[1] The time has now come, although, unfortunately for evangelicals, it is the liberal camp that has led the way.[2] Speaking in the context of types, von Rad writes:

> One must therefore—at last to use the controversial word—really speak of a witness of the Old Testament to Christ, for our knowledge of

Christ is incomplete without the witness of the Old Testament. Christ is given to us only through the double witness of the choir of those who await and those who remember.[3]

In an earlier part of his paper he says, "The Old Testament is indeed the picture book of a history of faith, and one of inexhaustible fullness."[4]

I have suggested that typology's principal features are correspondence, historicity, and prediction. It is the divine purpose that secures the correspondence, the linking of that which precedes to that which follows in the progress of revelation, but the divine design is no part of the typicalness. All scriptural events are divinely designed.[5]

The renewed recognition of typology is not a new exercise in the weird and fantastic. It is simply an outcome of the conviction that the God who spoke to us in Christ left His footprints, to use von Rad's figure, in Old Testament history. And one of the great values of the study is the fact that out of it comes a solemn warning to the exegete against finding in the Old Testament a testimony to a God who is not the Father of our Lord Jesus Christ.[6] Marcion should have been a student of the subject!

The extent of the correspondence between type and antitype is often large. At other times it is small. And in some cases the relationship is almost entirely that of contrast (cf. Rom. 5:12–21).

A final word about correspondence is in order. It is generally correct to say that the type is enlarged and developed in the New Testament fulfillment, due simply to the progressive nature of divine revelation. We are reminded of the remarkable statement of Calvin, "The Lord held to this orderly plan in administering the covenant of his mercy: as the day of full revelation approached with the passing of time, the more he increased each day the brightness of its manifestation."[7]

There are some questions that we should keep before us as we handle the Old Testament types and their New Testament antitypes. One of the first is this: To what extent did the Old Testament authors perceive that the things they were writing about were typical? It is generally agreed that their understanding of typology was very limited. But if that is so, then a second question looms before the interpreter: To what extent is it proper to find in the Old Testament a meaning that goes beyond the "authorial will" of the human writer? In other words, is it demanded that an exegete go beyond the historico-critical process to the theological perspective? Von Rad's words are worth weighing:

> We face the undeniable fact that so very often even the best "historical" exegesis is achieved from a theological point of view—that is to say, in the final analysis, from the side of the Christian faith. At what other place would Old Testament exegesis reckon with Paul's word about the veil (2 Cor. 3:7ff.)? At what point in its interpretive process does Christian interpretation think itself distinguishable from Jewish?[8]

A third question then arises: Should *we*—that is, we modern interpreters—follow the method of the Lord and the apostles in passages that they have not dealt with? Are we justified in finding Christ where they have not specifically found Him?

And, finally, what bearing does this have on the doctrine of inspiration? Let me phrase the question this way: If the New Testament author finds Christ in an Old Testament passage where the Old Testament author did not, must we say that the New Testament author has made a mistake? Does this phenomenon support the contention of some that the "phenomena" point to the existence of errors in the text?

Keeping these things before us, we turn now to the interpretation of our Lord's use of the Old Testament in John 13:18.

THE NEW TESTAMENT CONTEXT OF JOHN 13:18

After completing the prologue to the Gospel (1:1–18), the apostle John describes the manifestation of the Messiah to the world (1:19–12:36). Then he summarizes the response to our Lord's ministry (12:37–50). At this point the apostle shows how the Messiah revealed His messianic nature to the disciples (13:1–17:26). These five chapters are generally termed "The Upper Room Discourse." Lewis Sperry Chafer said that they contain "the purest Christian teaching we have anywhere in the New Testament."[9] In addition, he referred to the section as "the seed plot of all grace teaching," contending that every essential of doctrine was to be found in it, at least in germ form.

The opening thirty verses of chapter 13 are preparation for the instruction. The washing of the disciples' feet, a kind of explanation of the passion narrative,[10] is a vivid illustration of the ministry of Jesus in humiliation and exaltation, designed to motivate them to similar humble love by His self-abnegation (13:4–5 [10:15], 12–17). He later taught this truth more directly by the giving of the New Commandment (vv. 31–35).

The course of the narrative is interpreted by the words regarding the traitor. The truth of the preceding and following contexts does not apply to him.[11] Judas was a spiritual stranger in the midst of the assembly and, just as a jeweler puts his flashing diamonds on black velvet to accentuate their appealing beauty to the customer, so Jesus' act of humble love in washing the disciples' feet is presented against the black velvet of Judas's base treachery. Given a last chance to reverse his decision (v. 2), Judas nonetheless preferred Satan to the Savior. When the traitor's decision was clear (v. 27), the Lord Jesus remarked, "What you do, do quickly." It was "the voice of despairing love abandoning the conflict," but it was also "the voice of strangely blended majesty and humiliation."[12] The victim issued commands to the apparent victor! And finally, it was also "the voice of willing sacrifice" saying, in effect, "bind the . . . sacrifice with cords to the horns of the altar" (Ps. 118:27. The mention of the departure of Judas concludes with the words, "and it was night." Of this Augustine wrote, *Erat autem nox: et ipse qui exivit erat nox.*[13]

The opening words of verse 18 mark the change of atmosphere. Jesus' thoughts turned to the chosen ones. The verb "I have chosen" does not in this instance refer to election to salvation, but to the apostolate (cf. 6:70–71). The principle, no doubt, is involved, but the Scriptures usually ascribe the former to the Father. An ellipsis must be supplied before the ἵνα ("that"). Westcott suggests, ". . . *but* this has so come to pass that . . . (xix. 36)."[14] He had to be betrayed by human instrumentality; He had made no mistake (cf. Luke 6:12–16). The citation from Psalm 41:9 (v. 10 in the Hebrew Bible) is introduced as fulfilled in the betrayal—a breach of divine hospitality!

THE OLD TESTAMENT CONTEXT OF PSALM 41:9

Psalm 41 is a psalm that might be entitled, "Sickness and Suffering Amid Treachery." The content of the psalm suits the period of Absalom's rebellion very well. The faithless friend is Ahithophel, whose counsels were regarded by David "as if one inquired of the word of God" (2 Sam. 16:23). Apparently with the support of Ahithophel Absalom stole the hearts of Israel, and David, who had suffered perhaps from a lingering illness (there is no indication of this in the historical books), was forced to flee. The king must have known of the treachery but he did nothing about it. Delitzsch suggests that the reasons for his lack of action may have included (1) his love for Absalom, (2) his own sense of conviction over his deed of shame and bloodshed concerning Bathsheba and Uriah. At any rate, he left the matter of the conspiracy to God, conscious of his own guilt and sin (cf. v. 5). The fact that Ahithophel later came to an inglorious end and hanged himself heightens the resemblance to the New Testament picture of Christ and Judas (cf. Matt. 27:3–5).

Very briefly the flow of thought in the psalm is as follows:

1. The psalmist reflects on the blessedness of the man who is considerate of the helpless (vv. 1–3).

2. The psalmist records a historical plea he made when his enemies (vv. 4-8) and even his own familiar friend (v. 9) were against him.

3. The psalm concludes with a prayer for restoration and just requital for the treason (vv. 10–13),[15] and an expression of confidence in the messianic hope: "Thou dost set me in thy presence forever" (v. 12).

Two verses are of importance for us here. The first is verse 4, which plainly indicates that the psalm cannot be understood of Christ in its entirety. The second is verse 9, the one quoted in the New Testament. The blackness of the treachery is heightened by the reference to eating bread. As Perowne says, "The Oriental feeling as to the sacredness of hospitality would stamp such conduct with peculiar blackness. If David wrote the Psalm, the ingratitude was the worse, because of the honour conferred on one who was admitted to the king's table (2 Sam. ix. 10ff., 1 Kings xviii. 19)."[16] The metaphor of the heel suggests the kick of a beast.[17]

THE COMPARISON OF THE OLD AND NEW TESTAMENT TEXTS

NT	LXX	MT
(John 13:18)	(Ps. 41:9)	(Ps. 41:10)

IF: ἵνα ἡ γραφὴ
πληρωθῇ·

ὁ τρώγων μου τὸν ἄρτον ἐπῆρεν ἐπ᾿ ἐμὲ τὴν πτέρναν αὐτοῦ.	ὁ ἐσθίων ἄρτους μου, ἐμεγάλυνεν ἐπ᾿ ἐμὲ πτερνισμόν.	אוֹכֵל לַחְמִי הִגְדִּיל עָלַי עָקֵב׃

(Mark 14:18, 21)

ὁ ἐσθίων μετ᾿
ἐμοῦ....ὅτι ὁ μὲν
υἱὸς τοῦ ἀνθρώπου
ὑπάγει καθὼς
γέγραπται περὶ
αὐτοῦ·

IF: that the Scripture
might be fulfilled,

He who eats [or *ate*] my bread has lifted up his heel against me.	He who eats [or *ate*] my bread has lifted up his heel [lit. "magnified his heel," in the sense of lifting it high] against me.	He who ate my bread has lifted up his heel against me.

(Mark 14:18, 21)

He who ate with
me . . . for the Son of
Man goes as it has
been written con-
cerning him.

COMMENTS ON VARIATIONS IN THE TEXTS

John frequently cites freely from the Old Testament,[18] although the present quotation is nearer to the Masoretic text than to the Septuagint.[19]

There are some differences in the texts that we should note.
1. John uses τρώγων ("eats") for the Septuagint's ἐσθίων. Some think John used the former word, meaning "to gnaw, nibble, munch," in order to counter Docetic tendencies to spiritualize the concept of eating, especially in such verses as John 6:54, 56, 57, 58. It is found elsewhere only in Matthew 24:38; so it is for the most part a Johannine word. Perhaps that explains its use here.

2. John has the singular τὸν ἄρτον ("bread") as in the Hebrew; the Septuagint has the plural.

3. John's rendering of the Hebrew verb הִגְדִּיל ("lifted up") is freer than the Septuagint translation, for the latter is literal.

4. John's τὴν πτέρναν αὐτοῦ ("his heel") is different from both the Septuagint and the Hebrew, although elsewhere in the Septuagint the word πτέρνα is found as a rendering of the Hebrew word for "heel" that is used here. Thus John's word accords with other Septuagint usage.[20]

5. The opening of verse 9, "Even my close friend, whom I trusted," is not cited by our Lord or by John. The omission of the words may be intentional on Jesus' part, for it might suggest that He misunderstood the nature and character of Judas. That would call into question the omniscience of the Lord Jesus. It would conflict with the specific conviction of the Evangelist concerning the unique knowledge possessed by the Son of God (cf. John 2:23–25; 6:70–71; 17:12). The emphatic position of the pronoun μου ("my") before the word for "bread" may capture the emphasis on the breaking of table fellowship by a friend, without suggesting the error in judgment.

JESUS' HERMENEUTICAL USE OF THE OLD TESTAMENT

The citation is introduced by an introductory formula that also occurs in John 17:12; 19:24, 36, but nowhere else in the New Testament. It is, of course, from the mouth of the Lord. This citation and the one in 15:25 are the only two quotations of fulfillment *from Him* in John (cf. John 12:38; 19:24, 36; 19:28).

The use of the verb πληρωθῇ ("may be fulfilled") indicates fulfillment. It is a common misconception of casual Bible readers that when the New Testament states that a text from the Old Testament is fulfilled in the New, the use of the Old Testament text is that of precise predictive fulfillment. Thus readers are puzzled when they discover from a careful reading of the Old Testament that the Old Testament passage does not seem to speak precisely of what the New Testament seems to suggest. They fail to bear in mind the philosophy of the biblical authors. The writers of Scripture believed that God controlled history. Therefore, history of all kinds, especially the sacred record, spoke ultimately of the activities of the triune God. They did not think it necessary to define the precise kind of fulfillment found in New Testament texts, for it was God who controlled the prophets who wrote direct predictive prophecy and the other authors of Scripture who wrote of people, events, and institutions as types or foreshadowings of the future. Thus both kinds of material were fulfilled in the New Testament, although in a slightly different way. Speaking of typical messianic psalms referred to in the New Testament, Delitzsch comments, "All these psalms, not less than those of the first class [he is referring to directly eschatologically messianic psalms], may be quoted in the New Testament with the words ἵνα πληρωθῇ, with this difference only, that in the former it is the prophetic word, in the latter the prophetic history, that is fulfilled."[21]

What, then, is the clue to the precise form of fulfillment found in New Testament citations introduced by the New Testament authors as the fulfillment of Old Testament texts? It is the contexts of the passages. Only from an examination of the contexts of the respective texts is the interpreter able to analyze and define correctly the nature of the fulfillment claimed. In the case before us, it is clear from the statements made in verses 4 and 10, in which confession of sin is made, that the fulfillment cannot be directly predictive of Christ. It must be understood typically; it is a fulfillment of the Old Testament in a more indirect way.

There is, however, a significant new feature in the use of this psalm. Our Lord, using the psalm, refers the statement, not to Himself alone, but to His enemy, Judas. In other words, not only is the Messiah found in the Psalms, but other figures are found there as well. Nor is this an isolated phenomenon, as John 17:12 and Acts 1:16 indicate. What is the justification for this? Lindars explains it this way:

> Judas' treachery was extremely embarrassing to the early Church, and gave rise not only to a special work of scriptural exegesis, but also to a Judas-legend associated with it. (Mt. 27.3–10; Ac. 1.16–20). John here gives one of the texts used in this work. The argument is: Certain texts show that there will be a traitor; Judas actually was a traitor; therefore, when Judas betrays Jesus, *it is that the scripture may be fulfilled.* As before (12.38) consequence and purpose are confused. What is seen to have been inevitable by hindsight is represented as known by foresight.[22]

In my opinion, Lindars's explanation is full of unfounded and gratuitous assumptions.

The logic of the use of the Old Testament found here is far more penetrating and convincing. It is simply this: David prefigured the Messiah, i.e., he was a type of the Messiah. All would grant that. Thus it is perfectly natural and justifiable to see His enemies, too, as prefiguring the Messiah's enemies.[23] The unique end of Ahithophel by hanging, the very way by which Judas's life was ended, accentuates the God-designed typical relationship and supports the validity of the use of the Old Testament passage. In fact, Jesus' use of an Old Testament type may have been the pedagogical precursor of Peter's similar use of the Psalms in Acts 1:16. He learned his hermeneutics from the Lord, as should all of us.

A remarkable skill is exhibited here in the use of the Old Testament, which we ought not overlook. Of course, it is just what we might expect from the One who was the apostles' Master. In the first place, notice the reference to the eating of bread and its appropriateness here, since they were seated at the Passover feast. In the second place, as we noted above, the blackness of the treachery is heightened by the oriental feeling of the sacredness of hospitality.[24]

Treachery by one who received the victim's hospitality was particularly vile (and this was our Lord's table; He was the host). In the third place, David was a king, a fact that heightened the infamy of the deed against him. How much more heinous the deed against *the* King! Finally, the metaphor of lifting up the heel was taken from the figure of a beast's kick, some believe.[25] Under any circumstances it suggests "brutal violence" and is certainly a fitting figure of the betrayal that led to the cross.[26]

JESUS' THEOLOGICAL USE OF THE OLD TESTAMENT

The New Testament authors had a fully developed typology, one both deep and broad. History for them was *Heilsgeschichte,* salvation history, and it was all under the direction of the Lord God, who ordered it in such a way that it served the purpose of the unfolding of the divine plan of the ages. This illustration of the skillful use of typology points toward our Lord as the ultimate source of this practice among the apostolic writers.

There is also an evidence of our Lord's messianic consciousness. If Judas may be seen in the action of David's counselor, then the Lord must have regarded Himself as David's Seed, his Hope to come. This is, in fact, spelled out in the next verse (v. 19), in which, as Strachan says, "Jesus speaks the language of Divinity and is given complete Divine power even over this treachery (cf. v. 27)."[27]

The fact that Judas's treachery was, like Peter's denial, no sudden surprise to Jesus, we see that it "was not outside the horizon of God's providence"[28] nor beyond the divine foreknowledge of a Savior who knew whom He had chosen.

CONCLUSION

In the introduction I raised some debated questions, such as the question of the Old Testament authors' understanding of typology, and the extent to which it is proper to find in the Old Testament a meaning that goes beyond the "authorial will" of the human writer. These are difficult questions and demand fuller treatment than is possible in a chapter such as this. If, however, we may say, for the sake of discussion, that it is the general opinion of biblical exegetes that a strictly grammatico-historical method of exegesis, devoid of theological perspective, is the proper approach to the study of the Old Testament, and that typology was beyond the ken of the biblical authors, then it seems correct to say that there is more in the Old Testament than the Old Testament authors realized. One of our common statements to our students is this: "In interpreting the Word of God it is fundamental that we seek to find what the author meant according to the grammatico-historical method of exegesis." Though this statement is correct so far as it goes, it may actually be misleading due to a misplaced emphasis on the human author rather than on the author's words. Speaking of the use of Hosea 11:1 in Matthew 2:15, Edersheim writes,

> The words of Hosea were in the highest sense "fulfilled" in the flight to, and return of, the Saviour from Egypt. To an inspired writer, nay, to a true Jewish reader of the Old Testament, the question in regard to any prophecy could not be: What did *the prophet*—but, What did the *prophecy*—mean?[29]

Donald G. Miller, a rather sober-minded interpreter of the Word of God, has warned students of Scripture against engaging "in a process similar to lying on our backs and watching the clouds, seeing in them whatever elephants or giraffes or castles or faces our imaginations suggest to us." He also adds, "The clue to understanding here may lie in a distinction between what the prophet said and what *God* was saying through him. It may well be that God had more to say through the prophets than they themselves were aware."[30] I see no valid reason for thinking otherwise.

As for the question of whether we are justified in following the methodology of the Lord Jesus and His apostles, should we follow any other methodology of hermeneutics than that which they have taught us through the phenomena of their specific interpretations of the Scriptures? Can we not say, too, that just as Peter used the Psalms in Acts 1 concerning Judas in the precise way that the Lord used the Psalms to refer to Judas so those who follow the Lord should follow Him in His hermeneutical principles? If Peter learned his method from the Lord Jesus Christ, should we not do so too?

Hebrews 1:10–12
Indirectly Predictive
Messianic Prophecy

INTRODUCTION

The defense of the exegesis of the author of the Epistle to the Hebrews is not a popular task among Bible scholars today. In fact, learned antipathy to the epistle, prompted by contempt for its author's exegetical methodology, has characterized the reaction of scholars to those who would attempt a careful study of this unusual work. T. W. Manson, commenting on the use of the Melchizedek analogy in chapter 7 of the book, writes, "To support this proposition our author brings forward all kinds of arguments and performs the most amazing feats of exegesis."[1] "Far-fetched Old Testament exegesis and obscure Old Testament characters, such as Melchizedek, have little or no interest for us today," Neil adds.[2] "The exegetical methods that the author took over from the Alexandrian school," Moffatt firmly says, "are not ours."[3] Kennedy accuses the author of addiction to Philonic allegorical exegesis: "Our author is true to his training in his employment of the allegorical method of exegesis so characteristic of Philo."[4]

It does not require much reflection to see that these opinions are uniform attacks on the inspiration and authority of this book of Holy Scripture. And the onslaught continues. One of the most recent commentators, George Wesley Buchanan, writing in *The Anchor Bible* series of commentaries, claims, "Like other scholars of his time, the author was also capable of taking an Old Testament passage out of context and attributing it to the Messiah."[5]

Specific comments concerning the passage discussed in this chapter are almost as depreciatory of the author's exegesis. Sowers has suggested that the author did not read the text in its Old Testament context, but rather found it in a book of testimonies and cited it from that. That is supposed to account for his disregard for the context of biblical passages adduced as references to the Messiah.[6] And the renowned Oscar Cullmann asserts that the text of Psalm 102, cited here, really refers to God the Father, the Creator, rather than to the Son.[7] Cullmann, however, overlooks the fact that, while the eternal God is referred to in the psalm, the trinitarian distinctions are not mentioned at all.

There is a final question that we must deal with a little more fully in this chapter. It is one that I have alluded to several times in these studies: the question of the applicability of the New Testament exegetical methodology to our own study of the New Testament today. In a very perceptive article of a few years ago Richard N. Longenecker raised the question of the relationship of the descriptive and the normative in interpretation. The descriptive has to do with what exactly took place, and the normative with the relevance of past exegetical practices for today. The article concluded with this paragraph:

> What then can be said to our question, "Can we reproduce the exegesis of the New Testament?" I suggest that we must answer both "No" and "Yes". Where that exegesis founds itself upon a revelatory stance and where it evidences itself to be circumstantial in character, "No". Where, however, it treats the Old Testament in more literal fashion, following the course of what we speak of today as historical-grammatical exegesis, "Yes". Our commitment as Christians is to the reproduction of the apostolic faith and doctrine, and only secondarily (if at all) to the specific apostolic exegetical practices. Orthodoxy has always distinguished between the descriptive and the normative in other areas; *e.g.,*

in matters pertaining to ecclesiastical government, the apostolic office, and the charismatic gifts, to name only a few. I propose that in the area of exegesis as well we may appreciate the manner in which the interpretations of the New Testament writers were derived and may reproduce their conclusions via historical-grammatical exegesis, but we cannot assume that the explanation of their methods is necessarily the norm for our exegesis today.[8]

Of course, we must admit that we cannot hope to reproduce the content of revelation, for that was the unrepeatable sovereign activity of God through the prophets and the apostles. Nor should we abandon a careful grammatico-historical handling of the biblical texts. But I propose that the exegetical *methods* of the biblical authors are valid for interpreters today. And, furthermore, though we cannot claim the infallibility for our interpretations that the biblical authors could, since they were inspired authors, we must follow their methods. Since they are reliable teachers of biblical doctrine, they are also reliable teachers of hermeneutical and exegetical procedures. It is just this that is lacking in so much of our biblical interpretation today. Failing to examine the methodology of the scriptural writers carefully, and following too abjectly and woodenly the limited rules and principles of human reason's presuppositions, we have stumbled and lost our landmarks along the pathway toward the understanding of Holy Scripture. *Scriptura sui ipsius interpres* is the fundamental principle of biblical interpretation. The analogy of faith pertains to both doctrine and exegesis.

This final chapter deals with a different type of use of the Old Testament. I will use for an example the citation of Psalm 102:25–27 in Hebrews 1:10–12. We will examine the methodology of the inspired author with the hope that it may be of some help to us in our interpretation of other similar passages in the Word of God.

THE NEW TESTAMENT CONTEXT OF HEBREWS 1:10–12

A recent commentator has remarked concerning the Epistle to the Hebrews: "To study this Epistle is to be brought close to someone with a first-class mind abreast of its subject, who writes with an inner authority and who combines learning, originality and rigorous logic."[9] I certainly would concur, for the epistle is a magnificent composition, constructed according to a most carefully worked-out plan.

There are still many unanswered questions about the letter, however, such as When was it written? To whom was it written? Where was it written? and especially By whom was it written? Among the contenders for authorship are such illustrious names as Barnabas, suggested by Tertullian; Apollos, supported by Luther; Paul, the choice of Clement of Alexandria and others; and even Priscilla, the wife of Aquila. Harnack is responsible for the suggestion that Priscilla was involved in the authorship of the letter. It was inevitable that his theory, a bombshell in his day, should be revived in an age of feminism, and Ruth Hoppin has sought to do so.[10] However, the author refers to himself in 11:32, and in the reference uses the masculine gender.[11]

The author builds his primary thought around three great contrasts. They are like three concentric circles, and he proceeds from the widest and largest to the narrowest and smallest. First, the Son, the head of the world to come, is contrasted with the angels, heads of the old covenant age (cf. 1:5–2:18). Second, the Son, the new covenant mediator and head over God's house, is contrasted with Moses, the old covenant mediator and one dwelling in the house of God (cf. 3:1–4:13). And, finally, the Son, the High Priest after the order of Melchizedek and the new covenant, is contrasted with Aaron, the high priest of the old covenant (cf. 4:14–12:29).[12] The last section is the fullest, the doctrinal part lying in 4:14–10:18 and the ethical in 10:19–12:29. It is this Son of God who is the leader of the redeemed as they journey toward the city of God and the rest that He gives, which are to come (cf. 13:14).

After the introductory verses, in which the author contrasts the two great revelations, that in the prophets to that in the Son (1:1–3), he expounds the superiority of Christ as the mediator and head of the new covenant to the mediators and heads of the old (cf. 2:2). The fourth verse is transitional, and after it follow seven citations in its support. The first two explain the $\delta\iota\alpha\phi\circ\rho\acute{\omega}\tau\epsilon\rho\circ\nu$ $\check{o}\nu\circ\mu\alpha$ ("a more excellent name"), while the last five describe the meaning and force of $\kappa\rho\acute{\epsilon}\iota\tau\tau\omega\nu$ $\tau\tilde{\omega}\nu$ $\mathring{\alpha}\gamma\gamma\acute{\epsilon}\lambda\omega\nu$ ("better than the angels").[13]

We are interested in the sixth of the citations, taken from Psalm 102:25–27 (vv. 26–28 in the Hebrew Bible). The author cites the Psalms a dozen or more times.[14] It may have been his favorite book. The particular citation before us continues the author's emphasis on the fact that the Son is better than the angels. He is better because He is the eternal, immutable Creator. The citation is connected to the preceding quotation by a simple καί ("and"). The author draws a contrast between the creation and the Son's unchangeability. The opening pronoun of the quotation, σύ ("thou"), has been thrown forward by the author in order to emphasize the creative power of the Son, and that same emphasis continues in verse 11. In addition, in verse 11 the verb διαμένεις ("remain") is an intensive present,[15] stressing the eternal existence of the Son. Contrary to the affirmation of the scoffers of 2 Peter 3:4 ("Where is the promise of His coming? for ever since the fathers fell asleep, all continues [the same verb is used here] just as it was from the beginning of creation"), it is the *Lord* who continues, not the *creation!* As Moffatt says, "Nature is at His mercy, not He at nature's."[16] The words of Davidson are beautifully expressive of the exalted dignity of the eternal Son.

> The contrast between the Angels and the Son, in their respective places in the sphere of redemption is extreme. The former almost belong to the material world, assuming material shape and assimilating themselves to the elements of nature, as they serve God in His redemptive providence. The Son stands apart from the world and above it—being before it, for He laid its foundations; and after it, for He shall fold it up as a garment; and while it waxes old He stands over against it, unchanging.[17]

He is the one of whom Moses writes, and to whom we may flee: "The eternal God is a dwelling place, and underneath are the everlasting arms" (Deut. 33:27).

THE OLD TESTAMENT CONTEXT OF PSALM 102:25–27

Psalm 102 has been entitled, "A Plea for Help: Addressed to the Eternal God,"[18] and, "'My Days' and 'Thy Years.'"[19] There is some justification for its traditional classification as a penitential psalm. It is the cry of one whose sufferings, while finally unexplained, are nevertheless apparently related to his sins (cf. vv. 8–11, 20). His troubles are not only related to himself, but also to Zion; in fact, Zion's state may have contributed to his affliction.

The opening eleven verses contain the psalmist's plea for help. His lament is built on extensive use of previous psalms, indicating that he often resorted to the Scriptures to strengthen him in his spiritual life. The plea itself is reminiscent of Psalm 39:12; 54:2 (see also 61:1; 64:1; et al.). The lament is vivid, mentioning frailty, fever, wasting, pain, insomnia, loneliness, and despair. "A lonely bird on a housetop" (v. 7) is one of his figures that has become proverbial. I like "a pelican of the wilderness" just as well, for a pelican is a bird that seeks out the lonely haunts. The afflictions (vv. 3–11) are certainly adequate causes for the plea (vv. 1–2).

Things change with the emphatic וְאַתָּה ("But Thou") in verse 12. The psalmist, instead of bitterly contrasting his transience and changeability with God's eternity and immutability, draws comfort and assurance from the divine attributes mentioned, and to these he adds the important attribute of compassion. Since He is eternal, He controls time, and, further, His purposes are not necessarily accomplished in the immediate future. They have a long reach, stretching out to the end of the time. In verses 12–17 the psalmist, affirming that it is the time for God to act,[20] to restore Zion by His manifestation in glory,[21] looks ahead to the day when the nations will fear the name of God. In his eyes the prophetic prospect of the restoration of Jerusalem takes place simultaneously with the visible appearance of Yahweh.[22] (Cf. Isa. 40:1–5.) He is confident of the ultimate answer to his prayer (v. 17; 22:24). The honor of the Lord depends on it (v. 15).

Expanding on the preceding, the psalmist looks into the distant future and speaks of the restoration as the theme of the literature and of the praise of the generation to come (vv. 18–22). Again he refers the fulfillment to the time when "the kingdoms" serve the Lord (v. 22) and Israel is released from bondage (vv. 20–21). (Cf. Isa. 61:1–62:12.)

In the final section of the psalm, David renews his plea, drawing the same contrast between his frailty and God's eternity (vv. 23–28). Kidner comments, "This temporary darkening of the scene after the exultant spirit of verses 12–22 allows the last four verses to stand out in their full magnificence."[23]

We have, however, quite an interesting exegetical problem in the last few verses of the psalm, affecting the sense of the ones cited in the New Testament, primarily because of the different readings of verses 23–24 in the Septuagint version. The difference affects the way the Son is seen in the psalm. There are these options.

1. In the Hebrew text of verses 23–28 the speaker is the suppliant from the opening verse to the end of the psalm. That is the rendering found in our translations.

2. In the Septuagint, however, the translation is quite different. The plea of the psalmist comes to an end with verse 22. Then the Septuagint version, vocalizing the text in a different way, reads as follows:

> He [i.e., God] answered him[24] in the way of his strength,
>> 'Declare to me[25] the fewness of my days [i.e., admit
>>> that the set time for Zion's restoration is short]:
> Do not bring me up [i.e., do not summon me to action;
>> cf. Jer. 50:9; Ezek. 16:40] in the middle of my days:
>> Thy years are for generations on end.
> Thou, Lord, in the beginning laid the foundation of
>> the earth. . . .'

It is clear that the person to whom the words of verses 25–27 are addressed is said to be the "Lord." And, further, it is the Lord God who addresses Him. There is no other person than our Lord Jesus Christ to whom these words could be spoken.

Did the author of Hebrews understand the psalm in this way? That is another matter. From the use of the conjunction καί ("and") introducing the verses cited in Hebrews 1:10 one might conclude that he did. The "and" links the citation to the one made in verses 8–9, which, in turn, is introduced by the words πρὸς δὲ τὸν υἱὸν [λέγει] ("But of the Son *He says*").[26] That would seem to indicate that the author of Hebrews understood the words to be spoken to the Son and, since the following citation is introduced by the simple "and," that would mean that the words of Psalm 102 are also spoken to Him. It is doubtful, however, that the author's use of καί in the linking of citations together will support this strict application (cf. 1:5, 7–8; 2:12–13; 10:30).

The meaning of the Septuagint is somewhat obscure—an argument against its vocalization of the text. The Hebrew text is plain.

If the Septuagint is a correct rendering of the text, then the whole psalm is messianic, for the suppliant is called "the LORD." The sufferings, then, are sufferings related to the work of the Messiah, and references to the Kingdom represent His anticipation of the completion of His work with reference to the plan of God. The final words are the Father's reply to the Son, by which He declares that the universe will be superseded and the Messiah's servants will be faithfully preserved.[27]

I do not see how the doctrine of inspiration is threatened by this problem. It is possible, of course, that the Septuagint text represents the correct vocalization of the Hebrew text. In that case our New Testament would simply be following the correct text. If vocalization of the Hebrew text is correct, then the psalm, while messianic, is messianic in a different way. We will look at that in a moment. Further, a slightly different understanding of the New Testament author's understanding of the passage will be necessary, but that is consonant with the text.

THE COMPARISON OF THE OLD AND NEW TESTAMENT TEXTS

NT	LXX	MT
(Heb. 1:10–12)	(Ps. 102:25–27)	(Ps. 102:26–28)

IF: καί·

σὺ κατ᾽ ἀρχάς,	κατ᾽ ἀρχὰς σύ,	לְפָנִים הָאָרֶץ
κύριε, τὴν γὴν	κύριε, τὴν γὴν	יָסַדְתָּ וּמַעֲשֵׂה
ἐθεμελίωσας, καὶ	ἐθεμελίωσας, καὶ	יָדֶיךָ שָׁמָיִם:
ἔργα τῶν χειρῶν	ἔργα τῶν χειρῶν	[27]הֵמָּה יֹאבֵדוּ
σού εἰσιν οἱ	σού εἰσιν οἱ	וְאַתָּה תַעֲמֹד
οὐρανοί·	οὐρανοί·	וְכֻלָּם כַּבֶּגֶד
[11]αὐτοὶ ἀπο-	[26]αὐτοὶ ἀπο-	יִבְלוּ כַּלְּבוּשׁ
λοῦνται, σὺ δὲ	λοῦνται, σὺ δὲ	תַּחֲלִיפֵם
διαμένεις· καὶ	διαμενεῖς, καὶ	וְיַחֲלֹפוּ:

πάντες ὡς ἱμάτιον
παλαιωθήσονται,
[12]καὶ ὡσεὶ περι-
βόλαιον ἑλίξεις
αὐτούς, ὡς ἱμάτιον
καὶ ἀλλαγήσονται·
σὺ δὲ ὁ αὐτὸς εἶ
καὶ τὰ ἔτη σου
οὐκ ἐκλείψουσιν·

πάντες ὡς ἱμάτιον
παλαιωθήσονται,
καὶ ὡσεὶ περι-
βόλαιον ἀλλάξεις,
αὐτούς, καὶ
ἀλλαγήσονται·
[27]σὺ δὲ ὁ αὐτὸς εἶ,
καὶ τὰ ἔτη σου
οὐκ ἐκλείψουσιν.

[28]וְאַתָּה־הוּא
וּשְׁנוֹתֶיךָ
לֹא יִתָּמּוּ׃

And,

Thou, Lord, in the beginning didst lay the foundation of the earth. And the heavens are the works of thy hands;

[11]They will perish, but Thou remainest; And they all will become old as a garment,

[12]And as a mantle Thou wilt roll them up; as a garment they will also be changed. But Thou art the same, And Thy years will not come to an end.

In the beginning Thou, Lord, didst lay the foundation of the earth, And the heavens are the works of Thy hands;

[27]They will perish, but Thou remainest, and they all will become old as a garment, and as a mantle Thou wilt change them, and they shall be changed;

[28]But Thou art the same, and Thy years will not come to an end.

Of old Thou didst found the earth; and the heavens are the work of Thy hands.

[27]they will perish, but Thou dost remain; and all of them will wear out like a garment; like clothing Thou wilt change them, and they will be changed.

[28]But Thou art the same, and Thy years will not come to an end.

COMMENTS ON VARIATIONS IN THE TEXTS

The author, as is his custom, follows in the main the Septuagint text when it was still in its relatively pure "primitive" form.[28] But there are several significant variations.

1. The pronoun σύ ("thou") in verse 10 has been moved from being the third word (in A; fifth in B) in the Septuagint to the first in

the New Testament citation. The author made this change to stress the contrast between the Son and the angels, a contrast which the psalmist, of course, did not have in mind[29] (cf. Ps. 102:12–13, 27 [וְאַתָּה]).

2. In verse 12 the verb ἑλίξεις ("Thou wilt roll up") is found instead of the Septuagint's ἀλλάξεις, "change" (though LXX$^{A/B}$ have ἑλίξεις), possibly a reminiscence of Isaiah 34:4; ἑλιγήσεται ὁ οὐρανὸς ὡς βιβλίον ("and the sky will be rolled up like a scroll"). The change is not of significance for our purposes.[30]

3. The addition of ὡς ἱμάτιον ("as a garment") in verse 12 of the New Testament may exhibit the skill of a master of Greek literature, for the three clauses are balanced, each having a verb with a noun.[31]

4. The author's use of κύριε ("LORD") in verse 10 is important. It is not found in the Hebrew, although Hughes speculates that it was found in the text that the Septuagint translators were using.[32] The addition is justified on strong grounds. The whole psalm is an afflicted person's prayer of complaint לִפְנֵי וְהֹוָה ("before the Lord"), according to the superscription, and the object of the suppliant's plea is referred to seven times in the psalm as the "LORD" (cf. vv. 12, 15–16, 18, 19, 21–22). It is obvious that the "Thou" of the Hebrew text may be properly understood as "LORD," as the Septuagint has it.

THE HERMENEUTICAL USE OF THE OLD TESTAMENT IN HEBREWS

There have been various explanations of the reference of the text from Psalm 102 to the Son in Hebrews 1:10–12, although the word "Son," or an equivalent such as "Messiah," is not found there. Just what is the author's reasoning?

1. It has been said that the author of Hebrews was misled by the Septuagint's interpolation of κύριε ("LORD") and, since that was a common title for Christ in the apostolic age, he applied the passage wrongly to Christ. What would we then have to say of the author's inspiration? The facts from this epistle are contrary to this view. In Hebrews 8:8–12 and 12:5–9 the author does not refer the term to Christ.[33]

2. It was Calvin's opinion that the author accommodated the quotation to Christ *pia deflectione* ("by a pious deflection," or modification). I cannot follow him in this.

3. Quite a few commentators see the author as applying the passage to Christ by the logic of his opening chapter. In verse 2 he had spoken of the Son as one who was appointed heir of all things and as one through whom the Father made the ages. Thus any reference to the endurance of God would also be a reference to the endurance of the Son.[34] Hebrews 1:2–3 should then be connected with 1:10,[35] the former being justification for the address of verse 10.[36] There is, of course, some appeal in this view, but it is difficult to see how this would be convincing to Jewish believers, and the author was seeking to do just that—convince the Hebrew Christians of the supremacy of Jesus Christ.

4. I have already referred to the way the Septuagint interprets the last verses of the psalm. According to the Greek version, the psalm is a directly predictive messianic psalm. The suppliant is the Lord Jesus Christ, and the plea is the product of the sufferings He would undergo in the carrying out of His messianic task. It is an interesting view, but the obscurity of the sense of verses 23–24 according to this view make it a questionable one.[37]

5. There is a simpler view of the author's thinking—one that I find more satisfying. The author saw the psalm as christological for the simple reason that it referred to Yahweh as *appearing in glory* (cf. vv. 16–22). From the standpoint of his completed trinitarian understanding, he knew this appearance could only be the function of the Yahweh who is the Son (cf. 2:5; 9:28), an appearance already guaranteed by the First Advent.

We do the Old Testament believers an injustice if we suppose they never thought of the prophecies they heard or wrote. For example, when they heard that Yahweh would *appear* in Zion, they surely reflected on the significance of *seeing God*. They knew that to see Him in His unmediated essence was to die (cf. Exod. 33:20; Judg. 6:22; 13:22; John 1:18). Thus, the Old Testament believers could only live in some measure of puzzlement until the pieces of the doctrine of the Trinity were set in their proper places. Only the future could reveal which person of Yahweh (there are three!) would appear. The revelation of the doctrine of the Trinity solved their problems. When Jesus, the God-man, came, it became evident that *He* would appear in Zion at the Second Advent. So they interpreted the Old Testament from the standpoint of the completion of the divine revelation, finding in that book clear prophecies of Him that were only seminal to the Old Testament saints. The use of the Old Testament, then, is broadly, or indirectly, messianic.

Franz Delitzsch, in a discussion of the classification of the Psalms, calls this type of psalm "eschatologically Jehovic."[38] These psalms, of which in Delitzsch's view there are many, describe the advent of Yahweh and His kingdom through judgment. The fact that Jesus Christ would be the person of Yahweh to come does not lie directly within the view of these psalms. That Yahweh the Redeemer, when He should appear, would be a God-man was largely beyond the comprehension of the Old Testament saints. It is in the New Testament that the refinement of the Old Testament picture is found.

Without this insight many passages in the New Testament would be difficult to understand. With it they become clear. The principle of the author of Hebrews is one practiced by other authors, too. A careful study of such passages as John 12:39–41 (cf. Isa. 6:1, 10); Phil. 2:10–11; Rev. 1:17–18; 2:8, etc.). Oscar Cullmann is right, "We will reveal that the principle was an apostolic one. We have another instance of it in the first chapter of Hebrews as well (cf. 1:6 with Deut. 32:43).[39]

For lack of a better term I call this type of use of the Old Testament indirectly predictive messianic prophecy.

The Theological Use of the Old Testament in Hebrews

The author's identity of the name "Yahweh," the covenant name, with Jesus Christ, the Son of God, is a tribute to his high regard for the Second Person of the Trinity. In this, of course, he is in harmony with the early church. The apostles often make the identification (cf. Phil. 2:10–11; Rev. 1:17–18; 2:8, etc.). Oscar Cullman is right, "We should generally give much more consideration to the by no means self-evident fact that after the death of Jesus the first Christians without hesitation transferred to him what the Old Testament says about God."[40]

To be quite specific, the author of Hebrews affirms these things of the Son: (1) He is *creative* (v. 10; cf. v. 2); (2) He is *eternal;* the earth and the heavens grow old and wear out, like an old moth-eaten garment, but He abides (v. 11); (3) He is *immutable,* for He is ὁ αὐτός ("the same," 13:8; cf. Deut. 32:39; Isa. 41:4; 43:10; 46:4; 48:12), never to be supplemented or superseded. Luther rendered the line, *Du aber bleibest wie du bist* ("But you remain who you are"). Like the seasons and the law of gravity, He is unchangeable! He is exalted above all becoming. How foolish to continue in sin against an immutable God (cf. Job 9:4). And how encouraging to pray to a God who does not have the inconstancy of a chameleon, who does not change His thoughts toward us, who does not keep office hours and is not moody. His covenants and promises are unfailing, for He is faithful.

There is an ascending scale in the quotations of chapter 1. In the opening ones His name "Son" is stressed. Then He is assigned the prerogatives of a king and is called "God." Finally, the attributes of the LORD God of Israel are given to Him. That is the climax of recognition.

CONCLUSION

I think it is clear from a careful study of the exegesis done by the author of the Epistle to the Hebrews that it is not at all "amazing," as Manson says, nor "allegorical," as others say. It is sober, thoughtful, logical, reverent, and accurate. Further, it is a tribute to the author that his work, although not from the pen of an apostle, so far as we know, on its own sheer merit found its way into the canon of Holy Scripture.

> It is a tonic for the spiritually debilitated. The study of this epistle leads us beneath the surface of things to the profound depths of our evangelical faith, and enriches and establishes our understanding of the grace of God manifested on our behalf in the incarnation, self-offering, and exaltation of him who is the Apostle and High Priest of our confession.[41]

In conclusion I raise the question again: "Can we reproduce the exegesis of the New Testament?" Unhesitatingly the reply is yes, although we are not allowed to claim for our results the infallibility of the Lord and His apostles. They are reliable teachers of biblical doctrine and they are reliable teachers of hermeneutics and exegesis. We not only *can* reproduce their exegetical methodology, we *must* if we are to be taught their understanding of Holy Scripture. Their principles, probably taught them by the Lord in His post-resurrection ministry,[42] are not abstruse and difficult. They are simple, plain, and logical. The things they find in the Old Testament are really there, although the Old Testament authors may not have seen them fully.

In the final analysis the biblical interpreter is interested not only in what the inspired author meant but also in what God meant. Therefore, the New Testament understanding of the Old Testament is the true exposition of it, because it supplies the reader not simply with what Moses and the prophets understood but also with what the Holy Spirit understood, gave to them, and empowered them to write down. Adolph Saphir has an illuminating illustration of the matter:

> Supposing that there is a little plant before me. I can examine it. But supposing that I have a powerful microscope. I look at it, and now I can see a number of things which before were entirely non-existent to me. Have I put anything into that plant that was not there before? Have I changed the plant? Have I introduced my pet ideas into that plant? So, when we read Leviticus with the light of the epistle to the Hebrews; when we read the whole Old Testament with the light of the evangelists and the epistles, that is *exposition,* not *imposition* [italics mine]. We do not put anything into it. The Holy Spirit enlarges our vision to see what is there.[43]

Notes

1

[1]Max Black, "Induction," *The Encyclopedia of Philosophy,* ed. Paul Edwards (New York and London: Macmillan, 1967), 4:169-81.

[2]Benjamin B. Warfield, "The Real Problem of Inspiration," in *The Inspiration and Authority of the Bible,* ed. Samuel G. Craig (Philadelphia: Presbyterian and Reformed, 1948), p. 201.

[3]Ibid., pp. 223-24.

[4]G. B. Caird, *A Commentary on the Revelation of St. John the Divine* (New York and Evanston: Harper and Row, 1966), pp. 45-46. He adds a footnote, "The Hebrew word *tr'm* in Ps. ii. 9 almost certainly comes from *r"*, (to break) but by a different vocalization it could be derived from *r'h"* (p. 46). Mounce calls the vocalization "difficult," but says that may be a typographical error. See Robert H. Mounce, *The Book of Revelation* (Grand Rapids: Eerdmans, 1977), p. 106.

[5]John Calvin, *The Epistles of Paul the Apostle to the Romans and to the Thessalonians,* ed. David W. Torrance and Thomas F. Torrance, trans. Ross Mackenzie (Grand Rapids: Eerdmans, 1961), p. 61.

[6]John Calvin, *Commentaries on the Epistle of Paul the Apostle to the Hebrews,* trans. and ed. John Owen (Grand Rapids: Eerdmans, 1948), pp. 227-28.

[7]W. H. Griffith Thomas, *The Principles of Theology: An Introduction to the Thirty-Nine Articles* (London: Church Book Room Press, 1951), p. 136.

[8]Henry Barclay Swete, *The Apocalypse of John* (3rd ed. 1909; reprint ed., Grand Rapids: Eerdmans, 1951), p. 250.

[9]Many different explanations have been suggested for the identification of the name, from the sacred tetragrammaton, יהוה (YHWH), through "Jesus," "the Lord" (see Phil. 2:9–11), to an unrevealed name veiled from all merely human beings, which expresses the mystery of His divine essence, or the "hidden depths" of His nature. (See Leon Morris, *The Revelation of St. John* [Grand Rapids: Eerdmans, 1969], p. 230. Cf. also Mounce, pp. 344–45.)

[10]While the problem is not an easy one, $\beta\epsilon\beta\alpha\mu\mu\acute{\epsilon}\nu o\nu$ is probably the reading that best explains the origin of the other variants. We should render the word, then, by "dipped." See Bruce. M. Metzger, *A Textual Commentary on the Greek New Testament* (London and New York: United Bible Societies, 1971), pp. 763-64.

[11]R. H. Charles, *A Critical and Exegetical Commentary on the Revelation of St. John* (Edinburgh: T. & T. Clark, 1920), 2:133.

[12]Ladd's comments reflect a bit of uncertainty at this point. See George

Eldon Ladd, *A Commentary on the Revelation of John* (Grand Rapids: Eerdmans, 1972), p. 252.

[13]Derek Kidner, *Psalms 1–72* (London: Inter-Varsity, 1973), 1:50.

[14]Franz Delitzsch, *Biblical Commentary on the Psalms*, trans. Francis Bolton (1867; reprint ed., Edinburgh: T. & T. Clark, 1949), 1:94.

[15]James Moffatt, *A Critical and Exegetical Commentary on the Epistle to the Hebrews* (Edinburgh: T. & T. Clark, 1924), p. 9.

[16]Kidner, *Psalms 1–72*, 1:51.

[17]For a different view, see Kidner, *Psalms 1–72*, 1:53.

[18]Ibid.

[19]Swete, *Apocalypse of John*, p. cxl.

[20]Charles Augustus Briggs and Emilie Grace Briggs, *A Critical and Exegetical Commentary on the Book of Psalms* (New York: Scribner, 1914), 1:22.

[21]Charles, *Commentary on Revelation*, 1:76.

[22]Swete, *Apocalypse of John*, p. 47.

[23]Charles, *Commentary on Revelation*, 1:76.

[24]Charles writes, "As clearly as language can indicate, ποιμαίνειν and πατάσσειν in xix. 15 are parallels, just as ῥομφαία ὀξεῖα and ῥάβδῳ σιδηρᾷ in the same clauses are likewise parallels. It is noteworthy that in Latin *pasco* developed this secondary meaning also" (ibid.).

[25]One of the older commentators writes, "Instead of *bruising*, the Seer, after the LXX., has *tending*. Not by a sort of misunderstanding or arbitrarily. In the original passage itself allusion is made to the pasturing or tending; the word which signifies: Thou wilt bruise, differs not in its consonants, but only in its pronunciation, from that which means: Thou wilt tend. By this significant allusion it is indicated that the proper office of the anointed is to tend (Ps. lxxviii. 71, 72), but that upon their sinful quid pro quo, refractoriness instead of joyful obedience, a righteous quid pro quo follows on the part of the anointed. The double import of the expression could not be rendered in Greek; only one of the sides could be exhibited, and the *tending*, used with a kind of irony, has substantially much the same force as the original" E. W. Hengstenberg, *Christology of the Old Testament* (reprint ed., Grand Rapids: Kregel, 1956), 1:558-59.

[26]Swete, *Apocalypse of John*, p. 47.

[27]Reinhold Niebuhr, *The Nature and Destiny of Man: A Christian Interpretation* (New York: Scribner, 1943), 2:294.

2

[1]A. M. Hunter, *The Work and Words of Jesus* (London: SCM, 1954), p. 71.

[2]R. W. Dale, *The Jewish Temple and the Christian Church* (London: Hodder, 1896), p. 98; see also p. 228.

[3]I have seen this citation in my reading somewhere, but the closest thing to

it in van Ruler's book is the statement, "In what is said above I have not taken into account the possibilities opened up by the non-Reformed intuition that the OT alone is Holy Scripture and that the NT is by nature oral *Kerygma.*" See Arnold A. van Ruler, *The Christian Church and the Old Testament,* trans. Geoffrey W. Bromiley (Grand Rapids: Eerdmans, 1971), p. 95; see also p. 94.

[4]T. W. Manson, "The Old Testament in the Teaching of Jesus," *Bulletin of the John Rylands Library* 34 (1951–1952): 312.

[5]See Rudolf Bultmann, *The History of the Synoptic Tradition,* trans. John Marsh (New York and Evanston: Harper and Row, 1963), pp. 101, 104–05, 205.

[6]See D. G. A. Calvert, "An Examination of the Criteria for Distinguishing the Authentic Words of Jesus," *New Testament Studies* 18 (January 1972); Norman Perrin, *Rediscovering the Teaching of Jesus* (London: Harper and Row, 1967); R. S. Barbour, *Traditio-Historical Criticism of the Gospels* (London: SPCK, 1972).

[7]See R. T. France, *Jesus and the Old Testament* (Downers Grove: Inter-Varsity, 1971), pp. 22-24.

[8]Michael Wilcock, *I Saw Heaven Opened* (Downers Grove: InterVarsity, 1975), p. 25.

[9]Paul K. Jewett, *Man as Male and Female: A Study in Sexual Relationships from a Theological Point of View* (Grand Rapids: Eerdmans, 1975), pp. 116-17, 119, 134-35, 139, 145.

[10]Kenneth S. Kantzer, "Evangelicals and the Inerrancy Question," *Christianity Today* (April 21, 1978), p. 18 [902].

[11]Dewey M. Beegle, *Scripture, Tradition, and Infallibility* (Grand Rapids: Eerdmans, 1973).

[12]Gordon H. Clark, "Beegle on the Bible: A Review Article," *Journal of the Evangelical Theological Society* 20 (September, 1977): 265. This is a devastating critique of Beegle.

[13]Beegle's chapter on the phenomena (pp. 175-97) is intended to prove this, but even he hesitates to say the Bible contains "errors." He calls them "difficulties" (p. 176) and then concludes with an "if" statement that seems to reveal some doubt on his part (see *Scripture, Tradition, and Infallibility,* p. 197). Finally, on page 219 he refers to evangelicals who do not believe in inerrancy as recognizing "some errors" in the Bible.

[14]Ibid., p. 308; see also p. 151.

[15]Cf. Daniel P. Fuller, "The Nature of Biblical Inerrancy," *Journal of the American Scientific Affiliation* 24 (June 1972): 47-51.

[16]John Warwick Montgomery, "Biblical Inerrancy: What Is at Stake?" in *God's Inerrant Word,* ed. John Warwick Montgomery (Minneapolis: Bethany Fellowship, 1974), p. 24; cf. Richard J. Coleman, "Reconsidering 'Limited Inerrancy,' " *Journal of the Evangelical Theological Society* 17 (Fall, 1974): 207-14.

[17] The importance of the phenomena in constructing a doctrine of inspiration is not a discovery of the contemporary critics of inerrancy. Warfield discussed the matter years ago. See Benjamin Breckenridge Warfield, "The Real Problem of Inspiration," *The Inspiration and Authority of the Bible*, ed. Samuel G. Craig (Philadelphia: Presbyterian and Reformed, 1948), pp. 201-8.

[18] See C. H. Dodd, *The Interpretation of the Fourth Gospel* (Cambridge: Cambridge University Press, 1953), pp. 389, 257.

[19] Leon Morris, *The Gospel According to John: The English Text with Introduction, Exposition and Notes* (Grand Rapids: Eerdmans, 1971), p. 523.

[20] Ibid.

[21] H. C. Leupold, *Exposition of the Psalms* (Minneapolis: Wartburg, 1959), p. 592.

[22] J. A. Emerton, "The Interpretation of Psalm 82 in John 10," *Journal of Theological Studies* 11 (N.S.; April 1960): 329-32.

[23] Leupold, *Exposition of the Psalms*, pp. 594-96.

[24] Edwin D. Freed, *Old Testament Quotations in the Gospel of John* (Leiden: Brill, 1965), p. 63.

[25] See Emerton, "Melchizedek and the Gods. Fresh Evidence for the Jewish Background of John x. 34-36," *Journal of Theological Studies* 17 (N.S.; October 1966): 399-401; A. T. Hanson, "John's Citation of Psalm LXXXII Reconsidered," *New Testament Studies* 13 (July 1967): 363-67; M. de Jonge and A. S. van der Woude, "11QMelchizedek and the New Testament," *New Testament Studies* 12 (July 1966): 301-26.

[26] See Artur Weiser, *The Psalms* (Philadelphia: Westminster, 1962), pp. 556–61; Mitchell Dahood, *Psalm II: 51–100* (Garden City: Doubleday, 1968), pp. 268-71.

[27] J. N. Sanders, *A Commentary on the Gospel According to John*, ed. and completed by B. A. Mastin (New York and Evanston: Harper and Row, 1968), p. 259.

[28] See George Reith, *The Gospel According to St. John, with Introduction and Notes* (Edinburgh: T. & T. Clark, 1899), 2:49.

[29] J. H. Bernard, *A Critical and Exegetical Commentary on the Gospel According to St. John*, ed. A. H. McNeile (Edinburgh: T. & T. Clark, 1928), 2:368.

[30] B. B. Warfield, "The Real Problem," p. 140.

[31] See B. F. Westcott, *The Gospel According to St. John: The Authorized Version with Introduction and Notes* (Grand Rapids: Eerdmans, 1950 [reprint from *The Speaker's Commentary*]), p. 160; Bernard, *Commentary on John*, 2:368.

[32] See R. C. J. Lenski, *The Interpretation of St. John's Gospel* (Columbus: Lutheran Book Concern, 1942), p. 765.

[33] Bernard, *Commentary on John*, 2:368.

[34]Westcott, *Gospel According to John,* p. 160.

[35]Ibid.

[36]Benjamin Breckenridge Warfield, "The Biblical Idea of Inspiration," in *The Inspiration and Authority of the Bible,* ed. Samuel G. Craig (Philadelphia: Presbyterian and Reformed, 1948), pp. 238-39. Johannine usage, however, contrary to Warfield supports the reference of the singular   to a particular text (see 2:22; 17:12; 20:9; 7:38, 42; 13:18; 19:24, 28, 36, 37). For the Scriptures as a whole John uses the plural *graphai* (see 5:39). See also Bernard, *Commentary on John,* 2:368; Sanders, *Commentary on the Gospel According to John,* pp. 120, 260.

[37]Warfield, "The Biblical Idea," pp. 138-39.

[38]Ibid., p. 139.

[39]Ibid.

[40]Morris, *Gospel According to John,* p. 527.

[41]Warfield, "The Biblical Idea," p. 140.

[42]The Griffith Thomas Memorial Lectures, Chafer Chapel, Dallas Theological Seminary, Dallas, Texas, November 6, 1963.

[43]Morris comments on the anarthrous υἱός: "ʿΥἱός is anarthrous and sometimes this is pressed, but wrongly. This is surely another example of the definite predicate preceding the copula and therefore being with the article (see on 1:1)." *Gospel According to John,* p. 527. Evidently Morris is persuaded of the validity of Colwell's rule that definite predicate nouns take the article, if (as is usual) they follow the verb. When they precede it, they usually lack it (cf. E. C. Colwell, "A Definite Rule for the Use of the Article in the Greek New Testament," *Journal of Biblical Literature* 52 [1933]: 12ff.). Older grammarians, with considerably more validity than some contemporary grammarians and exegetes realize, argued that in copulative sentences, if the expressions are convertible, the article distinguishes the subject from the predicate. There are exceptions to both viewpoints. In the case here in John 10:36 the noun is definite according to either view, but the older grammarians would tend to see a little more stress on the character of the Son and not on His person or identity.

3

[1]Dewey M. Beegle, *Scripture, Tradition, and Infallibility* (Grand Rapids: Eerdmans, 1973), p. 237.

[2]Ibid.

[3]See Alexander Balmain Bruce, "The Synoptic Gospels," *The Expositor's Greek Testament,* ed. W. Robertson Nicoll, 5 vol. (Grand Rapids: Eerdmans, 1961), 1:75; Robert Horton Gundry, *The Use of the Old Testament in St. Matthew's Gospel* (Leiden: Brill, 1967), p. 210; Franklin Johnson, *The Quotations of the New Testament from the Old, Considered in the Light of General Literature* (Philadelphia: American Baptist Publication Society, 1896), pp. 292-93.

⁴James Moffatt, *The First Epistle of Paul to the Corinthians* (New York: Harper and Bros., n.d.), p. 117.

⁵C. K. Barrett, *A Commentary on the First Epistle to the Corinthians* (New York and Evanston: Harper and Row, 1968), pp. 205-6.

⁶Canon R. C. Walls, lecture in dogmatics, October 15, 1973, New College, University of Edinburgh, Scotland.

⁷Moffatt, *First Epistle to the Corinthians*, p. 116. Literally, punctuating the verse as two interrogatives, the text may be rendered, "I am not speaking these things according to human judgment, am I? Or does not the Law also say these things?" (NASB). The Greek word for "these things," ταῦτα, may also be written as ταὐτά (from τὰ αὐτά), in which case it would mean "the same things."

⁸Ibid., pp. 116-17.

⁹F. Godet, *Commentary on St. Paul's First Epistle to the Corinthians* (Edinburgh: T. & T. Clark, 1887), 2:12.

¹⁰Moffatt, *First Epistle to the Corinthians*, p. 117.

¹¹Archibald Robertson and Alfred Plummer, *A Critical and Exegetical Commentary on the First Epistle to the Corinthians* (Edinburgh: T. & T. Clark, 1914), p. 184.

¹²Ibid.

¹³Godet, *Commentary on First Corinthians*, 2:13.

¹⁴J. A. Thompson, *Deuteronomy: An Introduction and Commentary* (Leicester: Inter-Varsity, 1974), p. 250.

¹⁵Godet, *Commentary on First Corinthians*, 2:11. The words in Deuteronomy are an example of the humanity of the Law. C. H. Dodd, while admitting that the synoptic Gospels express an attitude to little children and animals that is very remarkable for that age, nevertheless contends that the early church had no appreciation for it and cites Paul's words "Does God care for oxen?" as evidence. He adds, "At least, the church was honest enough to tell stories and report sayings of its Master which transcend its own thought and practice, and remain a challenge to the church of later days. Here was Someone 'above the heads of His reporters', and the extent to which their best imagination could have invented the words and deeds attributed to Him must be strictly limited." Was Paul possibly "above the heads" of his commentators, too? Cf. C. H. Dodd, *The Authority of the Bible* (New York: Nisbet, 1929), pp. 227-28.

¹⁶See Leon Morris, *The First Epistle of Paul to the Corinthians* (Grand Rapids: Eerdmans, 1958), p. 134.

¹⁷W. L. Alexander, "Deuteronomy," *The Pulpit Commentary* (Grand Rapids: Eerdmans, 1950), 3:393.

¹⁸See Bruce M. Metzger, *A Textual Commentary on the Greek New Testament* (London and New York: United Bible Societies, 1971), p. 558.

¹⁹Moffatt, *First Epistle to the Corinthians*, p. 117; cf. Robertson and Plummer, *Critical and Exegetical Commentary*, p. 184.

Notes

[20]James Morison, *Matthew's Memoirs of Jesus Christ: or A Commentary on the Gospel According to Matthew* (London: Hamilton, 1875), pp. l-li.

[21]Robertson and Plummer, *Critical and Exegetical Commentary*, p. 184.

[22]William F. Arndt and F. Wilbur Gingrich, *A Greek-English Lexicon of the New Testament and Other Early Christian Literature* (Chicago: University of Chicago Press, 1957), p. 614.

[23]Ibid.

[24]Ibid.

[25]See 1 Thess. 2:20. The $\gamma \grave{\alpha} \rho$ implies an affirmative answer to the previous question.

[26]Anthony Tyrrell Hanson, *Studies in Paul's Technique and Theology* (Grand Rapids: Eerdmans, 1974), p. 164.

[27]C. F. Keil and F. Delitzsch, *Biblical Commentary on the Old Testament,* trans. James Martin (Grand Rapids: Eerdmans, 1971), 3:421-22.

[28]Benjamin Breckenridge Warfield, "The Biblical Idea of Inspiration," in *The Inspiration and Authority of the Bible,* ed. Samuel G. Craig (Philadelphia: Presbyterian and Reformed, 1948), p. 162.

[29]Hanson, *Paul's Technique and Theology,* p. 156.

[30]E. D. Hirsch, Jr., *Validity in Interpretation* (New Haven and London: Yale University Press, 1967), p. 125.

[31]Ibid., p. 61.

[32]Ibid., p. 126.

[33]J. I. Packer, "Biblical Authority, Hermeneutics, and Inerrancy," in *Jerusalem and Athens: Critical Discussions on the Theology and Apologetics of Cornelius Van Til,* ed. E. R. Geehan (Nutley, N.J., Presbyterian and Reformed, 1971), pp. 147-48.

[34]Donald G. Miller, *The Authority of the Bible* (Grand Rapids: Eerdmans, 1972), p. 67.

[35]Philip B. Payne, "The Fallacy of Equating Meaning with the Human Author's Intention," *Journal of the Evangelical Theological Society,* 20 (September, 1977): 243.

4

[1]L. Venard, "L'Utilisation des Psaumes dans L'Épître aux Hébreux," *Mélanges E. Podechard* (Lyon, 1945), p. 253.

[2]The importance of the present tense in the participle, as well as the proper meaning of the noun $\kappa\epsilon\phi\acute{\alpha}\lambda\alpha\iota\nu$ ("main point," AV "sum") must not be overlooked. The NIV has caught the force of the verse, "The point of what we are saying is this: We do have such a high priest, who sat down at the right hand of the throne of the Majesty in heaven."

[3]Donald A. Hagner, "The Old Testament in the New Testament," *Interpreting the Word of God,* ed. Samuel J. Schultz and Morris A. Inch (Chicago: Moody, 1976), p. 79.

[4]Nigel Turner, *Syntax.* Vol. 3 of *A Grammar of New Testament Greek,* ed. James Hope Moulton (Edinburgh: T. & T. Clark, 1963), pp. 325-26.

[5]T. W. Manson, "The Argument from Prophecy," *The Journal of Theological Studies,* 46 (1945): 135-36.

[6]The point may be illustrated by the fact that Hebrews cites Jeremiah 31 in both chapters 8 and 10, but each time the citations differ in certain details.

[7]"Gentlemen, do you have a Septuagint? If not, then sell everything you have, and buy yourself a Septuagint!"

[8]See Paul E. Kahle, *The Cairo Geniza,* 2nd ed. (Oxford: Oxford University Press, 1959). Important for New Testament study is the Palestinian Targum of the Pentateuch as found in Codex Neofiti and partially in Pseudo-Jonathan and the Fragment Targum. See Martin McNamara, *Targum and Testament: Aramaic Paraphrases of the Hebrew Bible* (Grand Rapids: Eerdmans, 1972).

[9]The literature is so vast that it is impossible to suggest anything other than a few books and articles to begin one's study of the subject. See G. W. H. Lampe and K. J. Woollcombe, *Essays on Typology* (London: Allenson, 1957); Francis Foulkes, *The Acts of God* (London: Tyndale, 1955); Claus Westermann, ed., *Essays on Old Testament Hermeneutics,* trans. and ed. James Luther Mays (Richmond: John Knox, 1963), a work containing several important articles on the subject; R. T. France, *Jesus and the Old Testament* (London: Inter-Varsity, 1971), pp. 38-82.

[10]Dewey M. Beegle, *Scripture, Tradition, and Infallibility* (Grand Rapids, Eerdmans, 1973), p. 237; cf. Arnold A. Van Ruler, *The Christian Church and the Old Testament,* trans. Geoffrey W. Bromiley (Grand Rapids: Eerdmans, 1971), p. 71.

[11]Robert Horton Gundry, *The Use of the Old Testament in St. Matthew's Gospel, with Special Reference to the Messianic Hope* (Leiden: Brill, 1967), p. 210.

[12]Brooke Foss Westcott, *The Epistle to the Hebrews: The Greek Text with Notes and Essays* (London: Macmillan, 1892), p. 200.

[13]R. W. Dale, *The Jewish Temple and the Christian Church* (London: Hodder, 1896), p. 162.

[14]Woollcombe, *Essays on Typology,* pp. 39-40.

[15]See France, *Jesus and the Old Testament,* pp. 39-40.

[16]We cannot discuss here such questions as the relation of typology to exegesis, allegory, and prophecy.

[17]A. Berkeley Mickelsen, *Interpreting the Bible* (Grand Rapids: Eerdmans, 1963), p. 236.

[18]See Dale, *Jewish Temple,* p. 61.

[19]H. A. A. Kennedy, *The Theology of the Epistles* (London: Scribner, 1919), p. 214.

[20]Adolf Deissmann, *Light from the Ancient East,* trans. Lionel R. M. Strachan (New York and London: Hodder, 1922), pp. 337-38.

Notes

[21]James Moffatt, *A Critical and Exegetical Commentary on the Epistle to the Hebrews* (Edinburgh: T. & T. Clark, 1924), p. 133.

[22]The word εἰκών (AV "image") has here the sense of *the manifestation of the reality itself,* "the illumination of its inner core and essence" (Kleinknecht, *TDNT,* 2:389). Kittel claims that the word in 2 Corinthians 4:4 and Colossians 1:15 indicates the equality of εἰκών with the original (Kittel, *TDNT,* 2:395).

[23]Philip Edgcumbe Hughes, *A Commentary on the Epistle to the Hebrews* (Grand Rapids: Eerdmans, 1977), p. 393. He comments, "The gospel transforms *anamnēsis* from a remembrance of guilt to a remembrance of grace!"

[24]Moffatt, *Commentary on Hebrews,* p. 130.

[25]Moffatt's note on the relation of the introductory formula of v. 15 to the citation from Jeremiah 31:31, 34 and the concluding words in v. 17 is apt: "The opening μετά γὰρ τὸ εἰρηκέναι, implies that some verb follows or was meant to follow, but the only one in the extant text is λέγει κύριος (v. 16). Hence, before v. 17 we must understand something like μαρτυρεῖ or λέγει ... or τότε εἴρηκεν ..." (Ibid., p. 141).

[26]Westcott, *Epistle to the Hebrews,* p. 317.

[27]The citation is from Psalm 39:6–8 in the Septuagint and from Psalm 40:7–9 in the Masoretic text.

[28]Thomas thinks that the author could not say that God does not "ask" or "require" sacrifices, since he has just said that God had commanded them (9:19f.), although it is no contradiction to say that He found no pleasure in them. Kenneth J. Thomas, "The Old Testament Citations in Hebrews," *New Testament Studies,* 11 (1964-65): 314.

[29]Hughes, *Commentary on the Epistle to the Hebrews,* p. 395.

[30]J. J. Stewart Perowne, *The Book of Psalms* (London: George Bell, 1864), 1:44-52.

[31]Even in the Septuagint the words are emphasized, although the structure of the verse differs from that of the New Testament citation due to the omission in the New Testament of the verb ἐβουλήθην.

[32]Thus Moffatt is wrong in saying that "body" is "the pivot of the argument" (*Commentary on Hebrews,* p. 138). See A. Nairne, *The Epistle to the Hebrews* (Cambridge: Cambridge University Press, 1921), pp. 74-75.

[33]The methodology of the author is reminiscent of the *pesher* method of interpretation (although, in my opinion, too much has been made of this in some literature). The Aramaic word *pesher* means "interpretation" (it is found about thirty times in Daniel as a noun or verb). The method of interpretation is of current interest because of its occurrence in the Qumran materials. In the Habakkuk Commentary, for instance, the author quotes the biblical text and then gives the interpretation with repeated references to words in the cited passage. The interpretation may be introduced by פשרו על ("its interpretation concerns"). We have something

very similar in Hebrews and in Paul's letters (cf. Rom. 9:8; 10:5-9). The author cites verses with accompanying interpretation, expounding the parts of the quotation that have relevancy (cf. Heb. 2:6-9; 3:7-4:13). Is this not, however what we should expect an interpreter to do in many cultures? See Simon Kistemaker, *The Psalm Citations in the Epistle to the Hebrews* (Amsterdam: Van Soest, 1961), pp. 65, 88, 126-27.

³⁴Franz Delitzsch, *Commentary on the Epistle to the Hebrews,* trans. Thomas L. Kingsbury (1857; reprint ed. Grand Rapids: Eerdmans, 1952), 2:153.

³⁵John Calvin, *Commentaries on the Epistle of Paul the Apostle to the Hebrews,* trans. John Owen (Grand Rapids: Eerdmans, 1948), pp. 227-28.

³⁶Westcott, *Epistle to the Hebrews,* p. 308.

³⁷William Manson, *The Epistle to the Hebrews: An Historical and Theological Reconsideration* (London: Hodder and Stoughton, 1951), p. 143; cf. Kistemaker, *Psalm Citations,* pp. 181-85.

³⁸James Denney, *The Death of Christ: Its Place and Interpretation in the New Testament* (London: Hodder and Stoughton, 1902), p. 234.

³⁹Westcott, *Epistle to the Hebrews,* pp. 307-8.

⁴⁰Ibid., p. 308.

⁴¹Kistemaker's comment that the author used the Septuagint text because it lent itself best to his interpretation, as the Qumran interpreters did, is based on the idea that he was primarily interested in the word *body.* We have seen that this is not true. Further, it raises questions concerning the biblical doctrine of inspiration, to which he has not addressed himself (see Kistemaker, *Psalm Citations,* pp. 87-88).

⁴²Benjamin Breckenridge Warfield, "The Church Doctrine of Inspiration," in *The Inspiration and Authority of the Bible,* ed. Samuel G. Craig (Philadelphia: Presbyterian and Reformed, 1948), p. 128.

5

¹E. W. Hengstenberg, *Christology of the Old Testament* (reprint ed., Grand Rapids: Kregel, 1956), 1:765.

²Names of the leaders include Gerhard von Rad, Walther Eichrodt, Claus Westermann, and Leonard Goppelt.

³Gerhard von Rad, "Typological Interpretation of the Old Testament." in *Essays on Old Testament Hermeneutics,* ed. Claus Westermann (Richmond: John Knox, 1963), p. 39.

⁴Ibid., p. 27.

⁵See A. B. Davidson, *Old Testament Prophecy* (Edinburgh: T. & T. Clark, 1903), pp. 229-39.

⁶Hans Walter Wolff, "The Hermeneutics of the Old Testament," *Essays on Old Testament Hermeneutics,* p. 185.

Notes

[7] John Calvin, *Institutes of the Christian Religion,* ed. John T. McNeill; trans. Ford Lewis Battles (Philadelphia: Westminster, 1960), II. x. 20 (1:446).

[8] Von Rad, "Typological Interpretation," p. 38.

[9] Lewis Sperry Chafer, chapel message at Dallas Theological Seminary, Dallas, Texas, September 20, 1950.

[10] C. K. Barrett, *The Gospel According to St. John: An Introduction with Commentary and Notes on the Greek Text* (New York: Macmillan, 1955), p. 363.

[11] Ibid., p. 370.

[12] Alexander Maclaren, "St. John," *Expositions of Holy Scripture* (New York: Hodder and Stoughton, n.d.), 2:191-94.

[13] "It was, however, night and he himself who went out was night."

[14] Brooke Foss Westcott, *The Gospel According to St. John: The Authorized Version with Introduction and Notes* (Grand Rapids: Eerdmans, 1950), p. 193. Turner suggests that the ἵνα should be taken imperatively, *i.e.,* "let the Scripture be fulfilled" (see 15:25). He does not like what he calls the "apparent fatalism" of John (Nigel Turner, *Grammatical Insights into the New Testament* [Edinburgh: T. & T. Clark, 1965], pp. 147-48). See also Leon Morris, *The Gospel According to John* (Grand Rapids: Eerdmans, 1971), p. 622.

[15] J. J. Stewart Perowne, *The Book of Psalms* (London: George Bell, 1864), 1:335. Perowne does not think verse 11 can be reconciled with "our better Christian conscience." But the punishment of treason is one of the duties of a ruler, to be executed under the hand of God who commissioned him.

[16] Ibid.

[17] Franz Delitzsch, *Biblical Commentary on the Psalms,* trans. Francis Bolton (1867; reprint ed., Grand Rapids: Eerdmans 1949), 2:48. Dahood translates the clause by "spun slanderous tales about me" (Mitchell Dahood, *Psalms: Introduction, Translation, and Notes* [Garden City: Doubleday, 1965]), 1:248. Few, if any, have followed him in this.

[18] Lindars comments, "The Hebrew and LXX have 'has made great the heel against me,' and the exact meaning of this is disputed (caused me a great fall by tripping me up?), and some editors suspect textual corruption. John's quotation is interpretive, and perhaps means 'has kicked me from behind,' i.e. treacherously (cf. G. B. Caird, *JTS,* n.s. xx [1969] p. 32.)" Barnabas Lindars, *The Gospel of John* (London: Oliphants, 1972), p. 454.

[19] Lindars says, "Again the non-LXX form of the text suggests that it has been selected in a Palestinian milieu," ibid.

[20] Edwin D. Freed, *Old Testament Quotations in the Gospel of John* (Leiden: Brill, 1965), p. 91.

[21] Delitzsch, *Commentary on Psalms,* 1:69.

[22] Lindars, *Gospel of John,* p. 454.

[23] F. F. Bruce, *Commentary on the Book of the Acts* (Grand Rapids:

Eerdmans, 1954), pp. 47-48; Delitzsch, *Commentary on Psalms*, 2:45-46.

[24]J. H. Bernard, *A Critical and Exegetical Commentary on the Gospel According to St. John* (Edinburgh: T. & T. Clark, 1928), 2:467-68. He writes, "To eat bread at the table of a superior was to offer a pledge of loyalty (2 Sam. 9[7]14, 1 Kings 18[19], 2 Kings 25[29]); and to betray one with whom bread had been eaten, one's 'messmate,' was a gross breach of the traditions of hospitality."

[25]See R. H. Strachan, *The Fourth Gospel* (London: SCM, 1941), p. 269.

[26]Bernard, *Critical and Exegetical Commentary on John*, 2:467-68.

[27]Strachan, *Fourth Gospel*, p. 269.

[28]Ibid.

[29]Afred Edersheim, *The Life and Times of Jesus the Messiah* (1886; reprint ed., Grand Rapids: Eerdmans, 1953), 1:215.

[30]Donald G. Miller, *The Authority of the Bible* (Grand Rapids: Eerdmans, 1972), pp. 64-65.

6

[1]T. W. Manson, "The Problem of the Epistle to the Hebrews," *Bulletin of the John Rylands Library*, 32 (September 1949): 10.

[2]William Neil, *The Epistle to the Hebrews: Introduction and Commentary* (London: SCM, 1955), p. 23.

[3]James Moffatt, *A Critical and Exegetical Commentary on the Epistle to the Hebrews* (Edinburgh: T. & T. Clark, 1924), p. xlvi.

[4]H. A. A. Kennedy, *The Theology of the Epistles* (London: Duckworth, 1919), p. 193. This opinion has received considerable adverse comment in more recent times.

[5]George Wesley Buchanan, *To the Hebrews: Translation, Comment and Conclusions* (Garden City, N.Y.: Doubleday, 1972), p. 22.

[6]Sidney G. Sowers, *The Hermeneutics of Philo and Hebrews: A Comparison of the Interpretation of the Old Testament in Philo Judaeus and the Epistle to the Hebrews* (Richmond: John Knox, 1965), pp. 6-8.

[7]Oscar Cullmann, *The Christology of the New Testament*, trans. S. G. Guthrie and C. A. M. Hall (London: SCM, 1959, 1963), pp. 234-35 (cf. p. 88).

[8]Richard N. Longenecker, "Can We Reproduce the Exegesis of the New Testament?" *The Tyndale Bulletin* (1970), p. 38.

[9]Hugh Montefiore, *A Commentary on the Epistle to the Hebrews* (New York: Adam and Charles Black, 1964), p. 3.

[10]Ruth Hoppin, "A Female Author of Scripture," unpublished lecture given at the Claremont (Calif.) School of Theology, April 2, 1974.

[11]The participle $\delta\iota\eta\gamma o\nu\mu\acute{e}\nu o\nu$ ("if I tell"; lit., "telling") agrees with the pronoun "me," which refers to the author. The pronoun itself is ambiguous,

being in form either masculine or feminine. But the participle determines the gender of the pronoun, and the participle is masculine.

[12] See A. B. Davidson, *The Epistle to the Hebrews* (Edinburgh: T. & T. Clark, 1882), pp. 23-25.

[13] James Moffatt, *A Critical and Exegetical Commentary on the Epistle to the Hebrews* (Edinburgh: T. & T. Clark, 1924), p. 9.

[14] George Howard, "Hebrews and the Old Testament Quotations," *Novum Testamentum* 10 (April/July, 1968): 211. The conclusions of Howard are not very solidly established.

[15] The verb may be accented as a present or a future, but both express the *Hebrew* future, or imperfect, equally well. See Franz Delitzsch, *Commentary on the Epistle to the Hebrews,* trans. Thomas L. Kingsbury (1857; reprint ed., Grand Rapids: Eerdmans, 1952), 1:81.

[16] Moffatt, *Commentary on Hebrews,* p. 15.

[17] Davidson, *Epistle to the Hebrews,* pp. 49-50.

[18] H. C. Leupold, *Exposition of the Psalms* (Minneapolis: Augsburg, 1959), p. 706.

[19] Derek Kidner, *Psalms 73–150: A Commentary on Books III-V of the Psalms* (London: Inter-Varsity, 1975), p. 360.

[20] Franz Delitzsch, *Biblical Commentary on the Psalms,* trans. Francis Bolton (1867; reprint ed., Grand Rapids Eerdmans, 1949), 3:115. He writes, "Thus, too, will He restore Jerusalem; the limit, or appointed time, to which the promise points is, as his longing tells the poet, now come. מוֹעֵד, according to lxx. 3, Hab. ii. 3, is the juncture, when the redemption by means of the judgment on the enemies of Israel shall dawn."

[21] The three verses preceding refer to the future quite clearly, so we are to take the two verbs in the perfect tense in verse 16 as prophetic perfects. The appearance in glory is still to come, but it will come. The rendering in NASB, "For the Lord has built up Zion; He has appeared in His glory," is incorrect. That of the NIV, "For the Lord will rebuild Zion and appear in his glory," is accurate.

[22] Delitzsch, *Psalms,* 3:115-16.

[23] Kidner, p. 362.

[24] For MT's עָנָּה the LXX has ἀπεκρίθη, reading the MT as עָנָה , "he answered."

[25] For MT's אָמַר אֵלָי the LXX has ἀνάγγειλόν μοι, reading the MT as אֵלַי אֱמֹר, "declare to me."

[26] The rendering of the AV is "but unto the Son *he saith,*" and the citation from Ps. 102:25-27 is then introduced by an "and" in verse 10.

[27] Kidner, p. 363.

[28] See Kenneth J. Thomas, "The Old Testament Citations in Hebrews," *New Testament Studies* 11 (1954-1965): 325. Thomas's article, built on a thesis of some years earlier, is a helpful summary of the textual background of the citations in Hebrews. The article is much superior to that of

Howard, cited earlier (note 14).

[29]Delitzsch, *Hebrews*, 1:81.

[30]See Buchanan, *To the Hebrews*, pp. 22-23.

[31]See Simon Kistemaker, *The Psalm Citations in the Epistle to the Hebrews* (Amsterdam: Van Soest, 1961), p. 27. On the text at this point see Moffatt, *Commentary on Hebrews*, p. 27.

[32]Philip Edgcumbe Hughes, *A Commentary on the Epistle to the Hebrews* (Grand Rapids: Eerdmans, 1977), p. 67. His view is possible, of course, but the majority of commentators would think it very unlikely.

[33]Delitzsch, *Hebrews*, 1:82.

[34]See Buchanan, *Commentary on Hebrews*, p. 21.

[35]See Otto Michel, *Der Brief an die Hebräer* (Göttingen: Vandenhoeck & Ruprecht, 1957), pp. 57–58.

[36]See Montefiore, *Commentary on Hebrews*, pp. 47-48.

[37]For a similar treatment see B. W. Bacon's "Heb. 1:10–12 and the Septuagint Rendering of Ps. 102:23," *Zeitschrift für die Neutestamentliche Wissenschaft* 3(1902): 282-83.

[38]Delitzsch, *Psalms*, 1:70.

[39]Vos comments, "There are also certain Old Testament statements of *Jehovah* which are in Hebrews referred to Christ, so that Jehovah becomes a type of Christ. These passages are Deut. 32:43, quoted in Heb. 1:6; Psalm 102:26-28, quoted in Heb. 1:12; Hab. 2:3, quoted in Heb. 10:37. From these references some again derive the interpretation that *everything* that is said of Jehovah in the Old Testament can properly be ascribed to Christ. The correct view, however, is that only the *eschatological* manifestations of Jehovah in the Old Testament may be referred to Christ. This is held also by Delitzsch. Only in these cases is Jehovah the type of Christ" (Geerhardus Vos, *The Teaching of the Epistle to the Hebrews*, ed. and rewritten by Johannes G. Vos [Nutley, N.J.: Presbyterian and Reformed, 1977], p. 61). I do not see how Yahweh (Jehovah) is a *type* of Christ in these passages. Yahweh *is* Christ in them. Otherwise Vos's comments are helpful.

[40]Cullmann, *Christology of the New Testament*, pp. 234–35.

[41]Hughes, *Commentary on Hebrews*, p. 1.

[42]For Christ as the "creative mind" behind the original and fruitful rethinking of the Old Testament, see C. H. Dodd's *According to the Scriptures: The Sub-Structure of New Testament Theology* (New York: Scribner, 1953), p. 110. He also acknowledges that the meaning of Scripture must not be restricted to that of the author, saying, "It would not be true of any literature which deserves to be called great, that its meaning is restricted to that which was explicitly in the mind of the author when he wrote" (ibid., p. 131).

[43]Adolph Saphir, *The Divine Unity of Scripture* (New York, Chicago, and Toronto: Hodder, 1895), p. 64.